From: The GG Collection - Love & Light!

Enterprise 2000

Greater Hamilton
Halton and Niagara
embrace the new
millennium

By

Michael B. Davie

Municipal Messages

In my capacity as the Mayor of Hamilton, it gives me great satisfaction to endorse this insightful book promoting our city as a great business centre.

Enterprise 2000 contains a wealth of useful and inspiring information on many of our city's most prominent individuals and companies. This informative new book also recognizes the City of Hamilton's historic and ongoing role as the hub of an economic region that extends well beyond our municipal borders.

Enterprise 2000 author Michael B. Davie has continued the momentum he generated with his earlier book Success Stories, and as co-author of Hamilton – Its Happening celebrating our city's sesquicentennial. Hamilton has much to offer and I never tire of praising this remarkable city. In this enjoyable task, I'm joined by *Enterprise 2000*.
- Robert M. Morrow,
Hamilton Mayor.

As Hamilton-Wentworth regional chairman, it is indeed a pleasure to commend Enterprise 2000 author Michael B. Davie for creating a worthy sequel to his previous book Success Stories.

Both books focus welcome attention on the many successful individuals and businesses driving this region's economy. As we enter the new millennium, Hamilton-Wentworth's population is steadily closing in the half-a-million people mark.

Hamilton forms the core of an international economic sphere that encompasses 120 million people within a day's drive of our city.

Enterprise 2000 casts a welcome spotlight on a region unlike any other.
- Terry Cooke,
  Hamilton-Wentworth Regional Chairman.

As regional chair of Halton region, I am pleased to welcome the arrival of this book promoting our regional community as a great place to live work and play.

The Region of Halton is within a 400-mile radius of some of the largest population centres and markets in North America. Halton's location near Toronto and the United States translates into expanded business and professional employment opportunities for Halton residents.

We enjoy a diversified economy and we're a leading centre for high-tech companies. Add in an abundance of parks – including the world-famous Royal Botanical Gardens – and you have a vibrant community filled with opportunities for a new generation.
- Joyce Savoline,
  Regional Chair, Halton Region.

On behalf of Niagara Region, I wish to extend congratulations to author Michael B. Davie and his new book, Enterprise 2000: Greater Hamilton, Halton and Niagara embrace the new millennium.

Here in Niagara, we are indeed embracing the new millennium and we eagerly await a future rich with promise and potential. Our region's diversified economy is growing. Tourism, always a strong industry in Niagara, is burgeoning with new investments and opportunities in the hospitality and tourism sector.

From soft fruit growing and winemaking to steel and other industries, Niagara has it all. Enterprise 2000 will spread this message to a wide audience.
- Debbie Zimmerman,
  Regional Chair, Niagara Region.

Acknowledgements

Inspiring. Intriguing. Insightful. Writing this book on the cusp of a new millennium has been a truly remarkable journey.

The stories of business and academia leaders are certainly inspiring. This book – the sequel to my Success Stories book - would not have been possible without their co-operation, support and encouragement. They, along with leading economic experts, lend substantial content and substance to my 60,000-word creation.

Also essential in the production of this fine book is the spectacular photography of Paul Sparrow. For a detailed description of his work and accomplishments, turn to his profile write-up in this book.

I'd also like to extend sincere thanks for the timely layout assistance and expert advice provided by Richard and Eleanore Kosydar of Tierceron Press. Thanks also to Eclipse Colour and Friesens Printing.

Cameron Guitard also deserves a special note of thanks for being so well behaved. Cameron is the baby model used throughout this book and is the son of my cousin Elizabeth Guitard and husband Randy.

Finally, my thanks and love to my wife Philippa who did much more than provide some great photos of Mike DeGroote. Her encouragement and unwavering support helped me through the pressures inherent in bringing a project like Enterprise 2000 from concept to finished book.

This artistic endeavour would not of been possible without the assistance of many supporters too numerous to mention. My sincere thanks to everyone who played a role in creating Enterprise 2000.
- Michael B. Davie.

Canadian Cataloguing in Publication Data:

Davie, Michael B.
Enterprise 2000:
Greater Hamilton, Halton and Niagara
embrace the new millennium

Includes index.
ISBN 0-9685803-0-0

1. Hamilton (Ont.) –- Economic conditions.
2. Halton (Ont.) – Economic conditions.
3. Niagara (Ont.: Regional municipality) –Economic conditions.
4. Hamilton (Ont.) – Biography.
5. Halton (Ont.) – Biography.
6. Niagara (Ont.: Regional municipality) – Biography. I. Title.

HC118.H36D38 1999
330.9713'52
C99-901151-0

Contents

About the Author

Michael B. Davie has earned a solid reputation as a veteran business writer with a flare for creating compelling profiles of innovative, successful firms across Southern Ontario.

The award-winning writer previously wrote Success Stories. He also wrote over 100 business profiles and come chapter text as co-author, with Sherry Sleightholm, of Hamilton: It's Happening, commemorating Hamilton's 150th anniversary.

Michael B. Davie is also an editor and writer with The Toronto Star, Canada's largest-circulation newspaper reaching millions of Canadian readers daily.

He has won literally dozens of awards for outstanding journalism and is a prolific freelance writer whose work has reached an international audience.

In addition to publications in the United States and Europe, his work has appeared with and without bylines in many major Canadian publications, including the Halifax Chronicle-Herald, Montreal Gazette, Winnipeg Free Press, Edmonton Journal, Calgary Herald and Vancouver Sun.

Prior to joining The Star, he was an editor with The Globe and Mail, Canada's national newspaper with coast-to-coast-to-coast readership.

Previous to The Globe, he spent 17 years as a reporter editor and columnist with The Hamilton Spectator, a big regional daily, which published thousands of his articles. He won 27 national, provincial and regional awards and citations of merit for outstanding journalism.

While with The Spectator, Michael B. Davie spent a decade writing for the newspaper's Business section where he wrote hundreds of inspiring business profiles. Hundreds of his articles have also appeared in American Metal Market, Iron & Steelmaker, North American Steel Journal and Marketing magazines.

Prior to joining The Spectator, the author spent five years working for other publications, including The Welland Tribune, a mid-sized daily where he provided business and political coverage as a reporter, columnist and editor.

Before The Tribune, he had served two years as regional news editor for one of Ontario's largest chains of community newspapers, the Brabant Newspapers Group.

His interest in writing began in childhood and as a teenage in the late 1960s to early 1970s his work began appearing in small, high school and counter-culture publications.

He turned professional in the mid-1970s as Editor of The Phoenix serving Mohawk College of Applied Arts & Technology where he earned a Broadcast Journalism diploma.

He also holds a Niagara College Print Journalism diploma and degrees in Political Science from McMaster University where he was repeatedly named to the Deans' Honour List and won the Political Science Prize for outstanding academic achievement.

Among the many journalism awards he's earned are several Western Ontario Newspapers Association awards for exemplary business writing. He earned his most recent WONA Business Writing award in 1997. The same year, he received, in Vancouver, a national Lifetime Achievement Award for journalism.

Born and raised in Hamilton, he currently resides in Ancaster with his wife Philippa and their children Donovan, Sarah and Ryan.

Michael B. Davie writes with the authority of a life-long observer of the Hamilton area business community – and the remarkable, dynamic success stories shaping its evolution.

Manor House Publishing Inc.

Opening Notes

Roaring, mist-shrouded Niagara Falls is where we begin to explore a vast economic region as it enters a new millennium.

Home to more than a million people, this economic region begins at The Falls and stretches around Lake Ontario, taking in Niagara, Hamilton-Wentworth and Halton regions before blurring into the Toronto metropolis.

At the heart of this expansive community is Hamilton with its Steel City skyline rising confidently from the southwestern tip of Lake Ontario.

The Ambitious City is flanked by the regions of Niagara and Halton which together help form one of the most diversified and prosperous economic centres in all of Canada.

As something of a sequel to my last book, Success Stories, this new book, Enterprise 2000, will examine the economies of the communities making up a vast economic region of more than a million Canadians.

It will also look at many of the successful business people and education leaders helping shape this vibrant region in the new millennium.

Enterprise 2000 will, however, take a somewhat more forward-looking approach. This book is more about the future than the past and we'll explore the ways that business leaders and a new generation are being prepared for the challenges that lie ahead in the second millennium.

We'll address the ways in which Niagara is further positioning itself as Canada's leading centre for tourism and entertainment. These efforts include the establishment of a permanent casino at Niagara Falls and the substantial investments in Niagara-On-The-lake by businesswoman Si Wai Lai. We'll also look at how John

Howard and the Niagara Land Company are saving and expanding Niagara's farmlands while also establishing a New World Culinary Centre in which the world's greatest chefs will provide advice on utilizing Niagara's own bountiful produce.

Along the way, we'll revisit Howard's castle-like home and we'll spend time with the manager, chef and winemaker at Howard's Vineland Estates winery and restaurant.

From Niagara, we'll travel west through Hamilton, exploring a city that offers much more than steel mills. Visitors to the Ambitious City are in awe of its parks and attractions. The vibrant city has low unemployment and a high quality of life.

> The Ambitious City is flanked by the regions of Niagara and Halton which together help form one of the most diversified and prosperous economic centres in all of Canada.

We'll visit a number of economic experts and leading business executives to explore what the future holds for Canada's Steel City. While the city's two big steelmakers, Stelco Inc. and Dofasco Inc. together provide 14,000 jobs, Hamilton's economy has diversified to such an extent that the health care sector now accounts for more jobs than the steel industry.

While in Hamilton, we'll catch up on the latest chapter in McKeil Marine's ongoing success story and we'll chronicle the growth of neighboring Heddle Marine. We'll also visit several other companies and examine Hamilton Laser Eye Institute.

Then, we're off to Halton for a look at this region's diversified economy and leading business success stories. These tales of business achievement include that of Tim Hogan and the down-to-earth approach he and his staff take when selling Mercedes Benz automobiles at Garden Motorcar.

Of particular interest is the inspiring story behind developer Rudy Reimer

and his family. Having built a number of impressive office towers in the Burlington-Oakville area off the Queen Elizabeth Way, Reimer has reshaped the area's skyline and made the area – dubbed 'Reimer Country' - more economically vibrant as a result.

Together these three Golden Horseshoe regions constitute a larger economic region with a diverse economy that includes everything from soft fruit growing and fine wines to heavy and light industry, high-tech firms, leading educational institutions and a seemingly endless population of entrepreneurs ready to embrace the challenges of a new age.

Among those entrepreneurs is Michael G. DeGroote who remains our most striking example of a local man who made it big and continues to conquer new horizons.

Barely able to speak a word of English when he arrived in Canada from Belgium at age 14, DeGroote went on to become a multi-billionaire and one of the world's richest men.

He's now forging a new business empire. We have full details in the Entrepreneurs chapter.

DeGroote's son, Michael H. DeGroote, is also a successful businessman. This developer is now involved in several prestige developments in Halton.

And there's a bio-profile on Tim Hortons co-founder Ron Joyce.

I'm also proud to advise that we have an entire chapter devoted to educational institutions and the ways in which they're preparing the new generation for the challenges ahead.

Given its role in educating tomorrow's business leaders, I've included Junior Achievement along with McMaster University, Mohawk and Sheridan colleges and Appleby, Columbia and Hillfield-Strathallan schools.

You'll find all of these stories and more in the chapters that lay ahead in Enterprise 2000. Enjoy.
- Michael B. Davie

The spectacular majesty of Niagara Falls .

- Photo by Paul Sparrow

NIAGARA

Gateway to Opportunity

The awesome spectacle of Niagara Falls has inspired daredevils, writers and lovers for centuries. It's also the dramatic entrance to a vast economic region.

The Niagara River takes on a determined sense of urgency as it nears the falls, rushing to the precipice, then plunging in a misty roar as it crashes into Lake Ontario.

This terrifyingly beautiful scene greets growing numbers of visitors to Ontario and Canada every year.

And it forms a gateway to the opportunity that lies just west of the falls as you enter an economic region encompassing over a million people in Niagara, Hamilton-Wentworth and Halton regions.

The first of these three Golden Horseshoe regions, Niagara, boasts a diversified economy that includes everything from heavy and light industry to commercial and residential development, high-tech firms and, of course, tourism. It's also famous for its soft fruits and fine wines.

"The Niagara Region is alive with new development as it enters the new millennium," notes Gregg Crealock, chair of the Niagara Economic and Tourism Corporation in NETC's latest annual report.

"It has grown steadily in recent years and is now poised to increase its share of Ontario's employment and economic growth," he adds.

Crealock and the NETC report suggest Niagara region is well positioned to achieve new levels of growth and prosperity.

"It has a heightened sense of its capacity to build an enterprising, balanced economy that is forward-looking, global in its outreach and aggressive in pursuit of development opportunities," he concludes.

The City of Niagara Falls went on something of a hotel development explosion in the late 1990s.

In 1998-99, a new 145-room Park Plaza Hotel employing 150 people was slated to open in the falls city.

The Peninsula Inn and Resort opened a $9-million, 19-room facility that is attracting a largely European clientele with its resort-like atmosphere.

The $65-million, 600-room Marriott Fallsview Hotel opened, offering an impressive view of the Falls from its location near the Minolta Tower.

Hotel development in the falls city also includes an 8-storey addition to the Skyline Foxhead hotel and a new 30-storey tower over top of the Days-Inn-Overlooking-the-Falls hotel.

During this time, a new, permanent Casina Niagara was established at Niagara Falls. This huge, new, $500-million casino facility contains 100,000-square-feet of gaming, a retail mall, a 350-room hotel and a 12,000-seat amphitheatre. The casino expects to gross $600-million annually and employ 5,000 people.

Niagara: Gateway to Opportunity

In the mid 1990s Casino Niagara exceeded all revenue expectations with 20,600 visitors per day. That number continues to increase.

The casino is another attraction in a city rich with attractions.

Although the warmer months are the biggest tourist draw, the annual Winter Festival of Lights attracts over 1 million visitors annually.

During the warmer months, visitors can view the awe-inspiring majesty of the falls from the newest member of the Maid of the Mist fleet, the Maid of the Mist VII that carries 600 passengers at a time across the churning waters below this world-famous attraction.

You can also while away the hours visiting the Lundy's Lane strip of tourist attractions, the Skylon Tower and Marineland.

The Niagara Falls City Centre commercial complex has brought 525 office workers into the city's downtown core. Factor Forms Niagara Ltd. has doubled the size of its Niagara Falls site and increased its workforce to 60 people. These developments come as poignant reminders that there is more to business in Niagara than tourism.

Indeed, business investment seems to be growing on a daily basis in the city of Niagara Falls, home to 77,400 people - and 14 million annual visitors.

And there are other signs of growth and prosperity in Niagara, a regional municipality containing some 410,000 people in 12 municipalities ranging in size from small rural communities to the city of St. Catharines, an urban centre of 133,000 people.

Nestled between lake Ontario and Lake Erie, just west of the Niagara River, the Niagara region is joined only by British Columbia's Okanagan Valley as one of Canada's very few regions' capable of growing soft fruits. The Niagara region is, in fact, a major centre for soft fruit of all types, particularly grapes that support the region's world-renowned wine industry.

Niagara's climate and geography allow it to produce world-class Riesling, Chardonnay and Pinot Noir grape varieties for premium wines meeting VQA (Vintners Quality Alliance) standards. All told, Niagara accounts for 80 per cent of Ontario's $215 million wine industry.

Fully two-thirds of Ontario's tender fruit growing lands are in Niagara region. Grape production alone accounts for 15,000 acres of farmland.

Niagara also boasts almost 1 million square feet of greenhouse space and the region's various greenhouses together employ over 2,000 people.

With a landmass of 1,800 square kilometres, Niagara region borders the United States and the region's four international crossings account for nearly 40 per cent of all international crossings between Canada and the U.S.

A study released by KPMG's Global Location and Investment Strategies Network ranked Niagara fourth amount nine municipalities when examining competitive conditions for developing and expanding new business due to its strategic location in the industrial heart of North America.

Niagara also features superb highway access with the Queen Elizabeth Way and a number of secondary highways running through its land mass.

Although Niagara's unemployment tends to be higher than nearby Hamilton's, it still boasts one of the lower unemployment rates in Canada. The region has a largely skilled labour force of more than 152,000 people. The government sector - school boards, hospitals and local governments - accounts for over 20,000 jobs.

There are approximately 13,000 businesses in Niagara region and 42 per cent of the region's products are exported, primarily to the U.S.

Major employers include General Motors of Canada, employing 5,200 people; TRW - Canada Ltd., employing 1,300; Atlas Specialty Steels, employing 1,100; plus Dana Canada Inc. and John Deere Ltd. which each employ about 1,000.

Other major employers include the region's media, consisting of daily newspapers St. Catharines Standard, Welland Tribune and Niagara Falls Review; plus numerous weekly newspapers, radio stations and cable television services.

The Niagara region is also a centre of higher learning, housing Brock University and Niagara College. The region is known for its parks, historic sites and gorgeous scenery.

Evidence of growth is everywhere in this region. Not far from the city of Niagara Falls, lies the city of Thorold, population 18,600 people, where employees at the Thorold office of Rolls Royce spent the late 1990s supervising the engineering, construction and commissioning of a $7-million plant for the London Health Sciences Centre.

Gallaher Thorold Paper doubled its production capacity in the late 1990s to 120,000 tonnes. Since 1998, the company has hired 185 people, bringing its total workforce to 325.

The border town of Fort Erie is also experiencing growth. The Fort Erie shopping centre underwent a $1.5-million addition in the late 1990s and a huge new Duty Free store opened at the Peace Bridge. Eurocopter Canada Limited, with annual sales of $76-million, announced an $11-million contract to export four helicopters to the U.S. Drug Enforcement Agency.

The Fort Erie Race Track, one of the most beautiful tracks in Ontario, has now been transformed into a major entertainment centre in this quaint community of 28,300 people.

Niagara: Gateway to Opportunity

- Photo by Paul Sparrow

Plying the waters of the Welland Canal, home to numerous vessels every year.

In Welland, the Rose City Plaza announced construction of a $1.8-million supermarket and plans for a $1-million addition.

Welland Pipe procured a $100-million contract to supply large-diameter transmission pipe for construction of a pipeline for Nova Scotia and New Brunswick.

Welland-based Niagara College invested about $3-million in establishing a Skills Centre for the Automotive Trades.

Commisso's Food Stores opened a new Welland store, creating 200 jobs.

Fantom Technologies, which manufactures vacuum cleaners in Welland, has been named by Profit magazine as one of Canada's fastest-growing companies with revenue growth of 769 per cent. Annual revenue exceeds $17-million. Tri-Media Marketing was recognized by Marketing magazine as one of Canada's top marketing agencies.

Welland-based Basic Technologies planned a $5-million expansion.

With a population of 50,000 people, Welland is famous for its busy canal system and the city is Ontario's second steel city.

On the outskirts of Welland lies the picturesque, leafy town of Pelham. Primarily a residential centre with a bustling commercial strip, Pelham has

seen an increase in residential construction with millions of dollars worth of new home construction.

With its main roadways sheltered by canopies of tree branches, Pelham - population 15,000 - is among the most pleasant places to live in Canada. It's home to many wealthy families: Average income levels here are well above the national average.

Rural, farming-based communities are found in nearby Wainfleet, West Lincoln, Lincoln and Grimsby municipalities. Of these, Grimsby, bordering Hamilton-Wentworth region is the largest of Niagara's rural communities and is home to 20,000 residents. Kittling Ridge Estate Wines of Grimsby has grown from 15 employees to 120 and added a retail store, tasting bar and patio to keep up with consumer demand for its wines.

The raw, rugged, roaring power of Niagara Falls.

- Photo by Paul Sparrow

Niagara: Gateway to Opportunity

- Photo by Paul Sparrow

Line-ups start early at the popular Shaw Cafe & Wine Bar.

Niagara-on-the-Lake has an enduring, well-earned reputation as Canada's prettiest town. It's also home to a new village community of 400 homes on 200 scenic acres.

This development is to architecturally blend in with Niagara-on-the-Lake's historic and picturesque town centre.

The community is home to more than 14,000 people and its beauty and serenity is attracting residential development, including the new King's Point, a 90-unit condominium complex

In other developments, Niagara College opened a $37-million campus at Niagara-On-The Lake and White Oaks Tennis World built a $2.3-million addition to its hotel and a $1.5-million conference centre. Peller Estates Winery built a facility employing 100.

Queen's Landing Hotel has undergone major renovations and expansions, nearly doubling the number of seats in its elegant Tiara restaurant to 220.

Businesswoman Si Wai Lai who has invested many millions of dollars in the community owns this world-class hotel and several other Niagara-on-the-lake landmark inns. In addition to restoring and beautifying a number of historic inns, Si Wai Lai commissioned the striking statue of playwright George Bernard Shaw, created by Ancaster sculptor Elizabeth Holbrook, which now forms a focal point in this scenic community.

Niagara-on-the-Lake attracts well over 3-million visitors every year, making it the region's biggest tourist destination after Niagara Falls.

Shaker Cruise Lines are now bringing tourists from Queens Quay West on Toronto's harbourfront to Port Dalhousie in Niagara. Some 300 tourists make each one-hour trip aboard Shaker's Lake Runner, adding significantly to the influx of tourists into the region.

Elizabeth Holbrook's statue of George Bernard Shaw surveys the street scene.

Niagara: Gateway to Opportunity

Lush vineyards can be found throughout Niagara region. These are at Vineland Estates.

- Photo by Paul Sparrow

Further west lie rolling vineyards and wine industry tours that provide ample evidence of the region's mixed economy.

In addition to its many vineyards, the region also boasts a number of vibrant shipping centres.

Niagara's bustling city of Port Colborne, home to 19,000 people, is also enjoying strong economic activity. For example, JTL Machine completed a $1-million project for the Stelco plate mill in Hamilton and

Niagara Shoes won a $1.6-million contract to make 53,520 pairs of gym shoes for the Department of National Defence. The German cruise ship Columbus now makes regular stops in Port Colborne.

Known as the Garden City for its flower-filled boulevards and picturesque streets, St. Catharines is the region's largest city with 133,000 people. It's also a major industrial centre and service centre, home to GM Canada and numerous automotive-related industries.

And business is booming in the Garden City.

A $400-million investment will allow production of a new generation engine and secure 2,000 jobs at St. Catharines' General Motors plant. The Gen III, a smaller powerful engine, is

being produced for light trucks.

Canadian Shipbuilding & Engineering Ltd., of St. Catharines, was awarded a $150-million contract to build five new forebodies for Great Lakes vessels at Port Weller Dry Docks. A separate $3-million contract awarded to Port Weller Dry Docks will secure employment for 400 people.

Canada's first Cool Climate Oenology and Viticulture Institute has opened at Brock University in St. Catharines. The $4-million Inniskillin Hall will attract people from around the world to learn about Niagara wines.

Further west is the municipality of Lincoln, a rural collection of communities, population: 20,000.

Driving Lincoln's population growth, in part, is its scenic setting,

Niagara: Gateway to Opportunity

flanked by Lake Ontario and the Niagara Escarpment. Add in a temperate climate, rolling hills interesting little communities such as Vineland, and you have a municipality growing numbers of people want to live in. This pressure for increased urbanization is at odds with efforts to preserve Lincoln's traditional role as an agricultural centre.

Countering this urbanization trend is Niagara Land Company, a partnership that is developing disused and underused agricultural lands into thriving vineyards and a New World Culinary Centre.

John Howard, an NLC partner is also the owner of Vineland Estates, a separate company offering fine wines and superb meals in a beautiful setting.

Nearby the NLC properties at Vineland, Ontario is Howard's 14-room, chateau style home complete with turrets and nicknamed Castle Howard.

This serenely-beautiful retreat is known for its bold decorating touches, including his daughter Erin's showpiece, round-walled, tower bedroom boasting famed, skater-artist Toller Cranston's wall-to-wall fantasy artistry. The walls match Erin's bed, also painted by Cranston, which features a twisting jungle of painted vines and flowers.

After acquiring Vineland Estates in 1992, Howard has done much to make it an even greater success. He's restored the estate's carriage house into a banquet room and added a superb patio restaurant to this property, known for its rolling vineyards and award-winning wines. A tower and rustic barn-store are more recent additions.

A genuinely thoughtful and gracious host, Howard's unassuming manner

- Photo by Paul Sparrow

Mark Picone with brothers Brian and Allan Schmidt.

and his insistence on giving credit to others, have made this creative and astute businessman a fascinating character study of success.

Among the more intriguing people in Welland is Dr. Tony Mancuso, an innovative dentist who literally puts his dentistry methods where his mouth is.

Innovation is also a hallmark of E.D. Smith & Sons, a long-established jams and sauces company on the Niagara Peninsula, not far from Niagara region.

In the same eastern Stoney Creek neighborhood you'll find Edgewater Manor, where fine dining is available in an elegant setting in an unusual building on Lake Ontario's shoreline. All of these businesses and more are listed in the Enterprise 2000 telephone directory at the back of this book.

Meanwhile, Howard, the NLC, Vineland Estates, Mancuso, E.D. Smith & Sons and Edgewater Manor all receive profile treatment, next.

Vineland Estates

Renowned chef Mark Picone wasn't sure what to expect when he arrived at Vineland Estates in the spring of 1996.

What he found was an abundance of local produce and meats, superb wines to accompany his dishes and the freedom to employ his culinary talents to the fullest at what is now one of Canada's finest restaurants.

"I'm very happy here," Picone says in an interview at Vineland Estates winery and restaurant. "I'm fortunate in that I've been given a free hand to do what I do best."

"I enjoy preparing meals to complement the many great wines here," he adds. "I also enjoy challenging the kitchen staff to come up with new suggestions."

Picone's arrival marked a pivotal point in the evolution of Vineland Estates, which traces its origins to a family-held mixed farm in the 1840s.

Hermann Weis, a 16th generation vintner from Germany's Mosel Valley, established the winery and much of the vineyards in 1979. Weis transplanted some of Germany's Riesling vinifera and is credited with playing a key role in advancing Niagara winemaking.

In the early 1990s the winery was acquired by its current owner-proprietor, John Howard, a former Xerox salesman who made his fortune after he co-founded the Canon dealership Office Equipment Hamilton.

Howard's initial business success came after merging with OE Canada; he added to his success in 1992 after Canon North America bought OE Canada.

It was then that Howard noticed Vineland Estates was for sale. He purchased the winery and vineyards at Moyer Road, Vineland, just a country mile away from his castle-like home.

Howard soon set about transforming the property into something truly special. He restored a century-old coach house and turned it into a dining hall. He created and expanded a patio restaurant. And he paid tribute to the efforts of others, erecting a plaque honouring the Weis family contribution to Niagara viticulture.

He would later transform a barn into an elegantly rustic retail store and build a five-storey tower offering sweeping views of his own rolling vineyards touching the edges of the forested Bruce Trail, with Lake Ontario and a distant Toronto skyline beyond.

> Howard has truly brought to fruition a vision of a memorable culinary experience in a setting of unrivaled natural beauty.

In the early 1990s, Howard's vision was a work in progress that would take the winery in new directions.

In 1991, Brian Schmidt had arrived at Vineland Estates to become winemaker at the fast-growing business, easing some of the pressure on older brother Allan who had served as general manager and winemaker since 1987.

The move meant Allan Schmidt, a founding member of the VQA (Vintners' Quality Alliance) board, was able to concentrate solely on the duties of general manager.

The sharing of responsibilities also enabled the winery to grow at a faster, smoother pace, building up to annual production of 30,000 cases by the late 1990s with annual production of 70,000 cases planned for 2001.

In the mid 1990s, the desire to bring the culinary experience to an even higher level had already captured the imagination of Howard and the Schmidt brothers, third generation winemakers whose family founded the Sumac Ridge Winery in Kelowna, B.C. The brothers also have had experience working in wine regions of Europe.

"For years, we were responding to the customers' needs and requests and we'd make changes every year," Brian Schmidt, 30, recalls, "and one thing people were interested in was a fine dining experience with great wines."

"We needed someone to make the fine dining experience happen – we knew that Mark Picone had returned from Italy," Allan Schmidt, 36, notes.

Picone was invited to prepare a dinner in the Carriage House for recipients of Howard's scholarship program which funds a university education anywhere in the world for staff members who exhibit consistently high qualities of diligence and service.

"That dinner was a confirmation," Allan Schmidt explains. "It reaffirmed the fact that with Mark we could improve the caliber of our restaurant. Mark had the experience and credibility to make our transition to fine dining happen. He raised the bar on our quality of cuisine."

The vote of confidence in Picone was well deserved and earned over a lifetime of involvement in the food industry. As the fifth of eight children in the Picone family of Dundas, Mark Picone spent much of his childhood helping out in the family store, Picone's Food, established in 1915.

Picone would later work at restaurants in Hamilton and Toronto to help cover the cost of earning a Bachelor of Commerce degree in Hotel and Food Administration from the University of Guelph.

By his early 30s, Picone was serving an informal culinary apprenticeship in Europe. He was in his mid-30s in 1996 on joining Vineland Estates.

"One of the things I like most about working here is the willingness to try new approaches," says Picone.

"We have the freedom to explore and develop our potential to the fullest."

➤ *Brothers Brian and Allan Schmidt flank Mark Picone at the Vineland Estates tower.*

Vineland Estates

Enterprise 2000

Dr. Tony Mancuso

When it comes to building great smiles, Dr. Tony Mancuso puts his method where his mouth is.

"If you want to look good – you're in the right place," the Welland dentist grins, his mouth widening into a full, perfectly white smile.

Missing from his open-mouth smile is any trace of silver fillings. All you see are natural looking white teeth.

The reason quickly becomes apparent. Mancuso, 39, has undergone the same method of dentistry he applies to patients: His fillings, like their fillings, are of white porcelain.

"I've had ten of my own fillings done this way and I no longer like to do the mercury or silver fillings," he explains in an interview at his office.

"Porcelain fillings are much better. They're bonded into the tooth with a chemical adhesive which holds the tooth together – and they look natural."

Although a porcelain filling is about four times more costly than silver, Mancuso finds the advantages of porcelain are well worth the higher price: Porcelain fillings are very durable, trouble-free and attractive.

"It's very normal for me to do porcelain veneers on an 80-year-old patient," Mancuso notes. "They should enjoy their last years on this earth and if they want to spend those years looking good, that's terrific."

"Aesthetic dentistry is very gratifying," Mancuso states. "The patients really appreciate the work that's done on their behalf. I'll never forget the time I improved the smile of an 80-year-old lady. When she got out of the chair, she flashed me a big smile and said I'd changed her life. I can't tell you how good that makes me feel."

The growing popularity of porcelain fillings and veneers is part of a wider trend of consumers opting for services related to cosmetic dentistry.

"I still have a family practice and I provide all the traditional dental services, from check-ups to root canals," Mancuso notes, "but the emphasis is on cosmetic dentistry."

"In fact," he adds, "almost everything I do now has some element of cosmetic dentistry associated with it."

Mancuso attributes the rise in cosmetic dentistry popularity to demographics and societal trends.

"The baby boomers want the California smile and vibrant health," he explains. "They want to look good and feel good for a very long time."

> "Aesthetic dentistry is very gratifying. The patients really appreciate the work that's done on their behalf… I can't tell you how good that makes me feel."

Mancuso believes one of the biggest societal trends shaping dental practices is the pronounced shift from needs-based dentistry to what he describes as "wants-based dentistry."

"In the past, there was far less emphasis on prevention of cavities," he recalls. "People didn't take care of their teeth to the extent many do now and a trip to the dentist tended to be out of necessity to see to a toothache."

"Now, there's quite a different phenomenon at work," he asserts.

"Now we're seeing people opt for dental procedures that are wants-based and designed primarily to improve the appearance of their teeth," he adds.

"People want to have a great smile. In the past few years we've seen a huge emphasis put on cosmetic dentistry."

Mancuso says baby boomers and a new generation of young professionals understand the importance many companies place on an attractive smile.

"Some service companies won't hire people who don't smile a lot. This reality and demographics are raising the demand for aesthetic dentistry."

From the beginning, Mancuso has understood and appreciated the role demographics play in dentistry.

Although raised in the city of Niagara Falls, Mancuso set up practice in neighboring Welland largely due to demographic trends in the Rose City.

"I researched the demographics and found a lot of older dentists who would soon retire," he recalls.

In 1987, Mancuso was just starting out when he purchased a practice from a retiring dentist and merged it with his own Thorold Road, Welland practice.

By 1990, Mancuso's practice had grown and he moved down Thorold Road to his current location: a century-plus older home with a major addition.

The office now has more than 3,000 square feet of space on the main floor, with second level offices and basement level staff lounge and laboratories.

The thriving practice supports a family that includes wife Debby and children Sarah, 13, Derek, 12, Caitlin, 7, and Matthew, 5. It also provides the progressive dentist with a strong source of professional satisfaction.

Among the innovations employed at his practice is the use of argon lasers to affix fillings and apply laser whitening.

Mancuso also uses computer software to digitally depict how a patient's teeth will look after a procedure.

"When patients get an advance look at results, it gives them confidence in the process," explains Mancuso who has taught scientific and artistic merits of smile design at seminars. He also conceived and developed Millennium Aesthetics – a live, hands-on program teaching dentists how to perform aesthetic smile makeovers.

Mancuso will continue to adopt new technology and dentistry approaches.

"I like to make extensive use of available technological advancements to create more benefits for patients."

➤ *Dr. Tony Mancuso takes an innovative and progressive approach to dentistry.*

Dr. Tony Mancuso

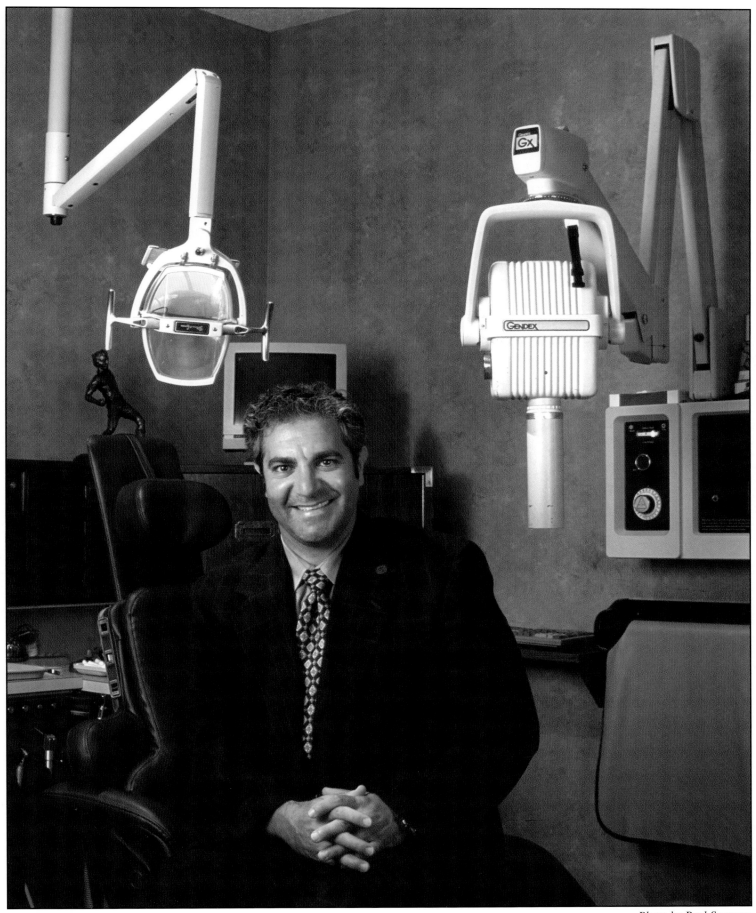

- *Photo by Paul Sparrow*

Enterprise 2000

Edgewater Manor

Rising like a castle on Lake Ontario's shoreline, Edgewater Manor is home to ancient architecture, exotic cuisine and grand dreams of entrepreneurs.

"I really love it here – and many of our customers have also fallen in love with this place," smiles Peter Trajkovski, general manager of the stately restaurant at the end of Fruitland Road in Stoney Creek.

"It's beautiful here, truly out of the ordinary," notes Trajkovski, 27, also a co-owner of the restaurant with his father Alex and partner Terry Terpoy.

"And," he adds, "we hope every visitor has a memorable experience."

Indeed, with a sweeping view of Lake Ontario, a tranquil, park-like setting and a building steeped in history, it's a virtual certainty that any visit to Edgewater Manor will be rendered unforgettable.

From the moment you arrive, it's impossible not to be charmed and captivated by the building's ornate manor house exterior reminiscent of medieval Europe and colonial Canada.

The imposing yet inviting structure offers an imaginative blend of several architectural styles giving the unique building an aura of subdued grandeur and understated elegance.

Inside, you can pour over a menu featuring everything from steak and lobster to Chef Ken Lefebour's Manorbriand specialty and exotic fare such as ostrich and seared caribou.

You can also select from one of the most extensive wine lists in Ontario while enjoying the sounds of an acoustic guitarist or jazz ensemble.

And you can bask in a grand yet homey atmosphere resplendent with surroundings of ornate woodwork, fireplaces, stained glass windows and a marble staircase from the 1700s.

It's the stuff that dreams are made of. But it wasn't always that way: When Trajkovski discovered the building in 1995 it was badly rundown. Weeds and thickets engulfed the property. Mounds of garbage obscured the view of the lake. The roadway and lands were little more than an illegal dump.

"I know some people thought we were crazy for buying it," Trajkovski recalls. "But I had a vision of the home's potential. I saw its hidden beauty right away. To me, it was like a diamond in the rough. I knew what it could be. It would be beautiful again."

> "I know some people thought we were crazy for buying it. But I had a vision of the home's potential. I saw its hidden beauty right away... I knew what it could be. It would be beautiful again."

The building was repaired and renovated from October 1995 to July 1996. The partnership also opened a second restaurant in 1998, the Terrace on the Green, opposite the Lion's Head golf course in Brampton.

Alex Trajkovski and Terry Terpoy manage this restaurant while Peter Trajkovski oversees Edgewater Manor.

Although still in his 20s, Trajkovski brings many years of experience to his general manager role. His family has long been involved in the restaurant business. Trajkovski spent much of his youth working as a busboy, waiter and bartender in many of the family's former restaurants, including Gatsby's and The Old Barber House.

In restoring Edgewater Manor to its former splendour, Trajkovski became fascinated with the building's history.

Phillip Reginald Morris, a lawyer and stock market investor, constructed it in the early 1920s. But much of the structure predates this era, as Morris was fond of salvaging and reusing whole sections of older buildings that had been torn down. To look at Edgewater Manor today is to see remnants of the past, sections of Hamilton's old post office and TH&B Railway station from the 1800s. The staircase dating to the 1700s previously belonged to a bank in Toronto. Tile and marble work from England and Europe is even older.

The success Phillip Morris had enjoyed didn't last long enough for him to complete his home. The 1929 stock market crash wiped out his fortune.

His house remained an empty shell until 1948 when son Alan Morris took over the structure and completed it, turning it into an apartment house.

In 1956, Philip Morris and wife Jean moved into one of the apartments. Philip Morris was finally residing in the home of his dreams.

The Morris family sold the house in 1971 and it continued to be used as a small apartment house until it eventually fell into disrepair.

After acquiring and restoring the house in 1995, Trajkovski successfully recaptured much of the home's original splendour. He's also added a 100-seat dining room addition known as the Morris Room in honour of the home's original dreamer/builder.

Groups can reserve smaller dining rooms seating 10-30 people. All rooms boast fireplaces, high-backed chairs and views of Lake Ontario. An outdoor patio was planned for opening in 2000.

In a move that puzzled rivals, Trajkovski converted a dining room into a lounge, losing 50 dining seats.

"Competitors have asked how I can give up 50 seats," Trajkovski notes while his lovebirds Romeo and Juliet chatter happily in the background.

"But I want to keep our capacity at 170 seats so our chef and staff can apply a more personal touch," he adds.

"It means we can all devote a little more time to making everyone's visit here as enjoyable as possible."

➤ *Peter Trajkovski became fascinated with Edgewater Manor's rich history and eclectic architecture.*

Edgewater Manor

- *Photo by Paul Sparrow*

Enterprise 2000

E. D. Smith & Sons, Limited

A small store is granting a welcome glimpse into the inspiring legacy of jam-maker E.D. Smith & Sons.

Tucked away in a 1850s-era stone building off Highway 8 in Stoney Creek, the aptly named Heritage Shoppe literally offers a taste of the legendary family firm's products.

Wander into this country store on the E.D. Smith property, and you become captivated by the enticing aroma of freshly baked pies stuffed with the company's famous fillings.

You can also buy an assortment of jams plus such specialty treats as chocolate-covered fruits, tarts, hard and soft yogurt dishes, parfaits and freshly squeezed juices. Although the specialty items are available only in the store, the company isn't ruling out the possibility of one day producing some of these items in mass quantities if consumer demand warrants this move.

All of the store's many treats can be enjoyed in a warm, rustic atmosphere. The building still boasts its original stonework, and hand-hewn wooden beams bolster the structure's colonial Canadian charm. A nearby 1949 steam jacketed kettle and other memorabilia add to the building's sense of history.

You can also peruse the store's archival display of Smith family record books, diaries and photographs.

Of particular interest is a book tracing the Smith family's fascinating history. The 264-page book, *The House That Jam Built*, was written by company president Llewellyn S. Smith and is the result of years of painstaking research. It has a wealth of data on generations of this pioneering family enterprise.

With its location near Fruitland Road in Stoney Creek's Winona community, not far from the Niagara region border,

the Heritage Shoppe will be the first featured stop for many Niagara tours.

Visitors can browse the Heritage Shoppe – run by Llewellyn Smith's wife Susan - pick their own fruits or enjoy picnic lunches on the property.

The E.D. Smith Fruit Farms, Inc. division grows sweet and sour cherries, strawberries, raspberries, peaches, pears, apples and plums on 200 acres of land, mainly at the Stoney Creek farm site, with remaining acreage at farms in east Winona and Vineland.

These farms supply roadside stands, the Heritage Shoppe, wholesale markets and a pick-your-own-fruits business drawing 15,000 people annually. The company is investing $3.5 million to expand, upgrade and replant its lands.

… The House That Jam Built was written by company president Llewellyn S. Smith and is the result of years of painstaking research.

Company President Llewellyn S. Smith observes that his *House That Jam Built* book and the Heritage Shoppe support a business strategy that will take the company into the new millennium. "We're taking a three pronged approach," Smith points out.

"First," he adds, "we're looking to meet the needs of the growing agri-tourism market by taking greater advantage of our location as the first major farm business on the Niagara gateway. The Heritage Shoppe is a key part of this approach."

"Secondly," he continues, "we're working as well to build our brand identification in the marketplace."

"Finally," Smith concludes, "we're committed to a long-term investment in land to meet the need for fruit production. We'll expand to 245 acres."

E.D. Smith's manufacturing business is bustling. By 1999, annual sales surpassed $125 million. Production approached 7 million 12-bottle cases.

About 40 per cent of the business is devoted to production of tomato-based

pasta, pizza and salsa sauces. Another 40 per cent serves markets for jams, pie fillings and fruit toppings while the remaining 20 per cent is dedicated to specialty sauces and syrups.

E.D. Smith is Canada's largest maker of jam products and has a 15 per cent share of the market under its own label. The company also has the largest share of the retail canned pie fillings market.

Much of the company's production is sold to wholesalers, restaurants and the private label retail sector.

E.D. Smith products are marketed under a number of private labels. It also produces H.P. Sauce and imports and distributes world famous Lea & Perrins Worcestershire Sauce.

The firm now boasts 385 employees. Manufacturing space has grown to 150,000 square feet. Warehouse space is now 250,000 square feet and office space is 26,000 square feet.

Smith notes the company's success is built on a family history that began over two centuries ago when Silas Smith left the U.S. for Canada in 1787.

In 1875 Ernest D'Israeli Smith, a fourth generation Smith, started a fruit farm and in 1882, formed the company.

As the company grew through successive generations, it has never lost sight of its traditional, founding values.

"Our people operate with values that include honesty, fairness, persistence, trust, teamwork, personal development and recognition," Smith notes.

"We apply these values to our policies, procedures, personnel appraisals, our customers and our whole way of doing business," he adds.

"We'll continue to operate within our values and grow while remaining an independent, Canadian-owned family enterprise."

➤ *E.D. Smith's Llewellyn Smith, Lesleyann Cook, Linda McNulty and Laura Inglis welcome visitors to the Heritage Shoppe.*

E. D. Smith & Sons, Limited

- Photo by Paul Sparrow

Enterprise 2000

Niagara Land Company

The world's best chefs will feature Niagara's finest food and wines at the New World Culinary Centre.

Slated for completion by the fall of 2000, the New World Culinary Centre will house a 20,000 square foot winery and restaurant.

As well, the centre will contain a 10,000 square foot greenhouse where local produce will be grown.

The spacious greenhouse will also serve as a backdrop to a 500-seat amphitheatre where the world's greatest chefs will appear on screen via satellite transmissions to demonstrate meal preparations and cooking tips using flown-in Ontario produce.

Visitors will have an opportunity to take part in working in the vineyard, winery and kitchen to enhance their understanding and appreciation for the care taken in preparing great wines and foods. A 56-room chalet-style inn offers overnight accommodations.

Situated on the Niagara bench, a sloping plateau halfway up the Niagara escarpment at Vineland, the centre off Cherry Avenue will sit on a 275-acre site almost entirely consisting of lush, gently sloping vineyards.

In fact, the site features the largest single planting of European grape stock in North America. All told, 325,000 new grape vines have been planted, compared with 45,000 at nearby Vineland Estates.

Despite its size, the centre itself will take up little of the land as it is to be built into the hillside and will be partly underground. The building will offer stunning views of Niagara Falls and the Toronto skyline. Patrons will also be able to dine amid oak caskets and barrels in the centre's restaurant.

The ambitious project is an exciting undertaking for the Niagara Land Company, a little-known firm that is shaping the destiny of the regional wine and food industries.

"We grow some of the best fruit and vegetables, some of the best materials for great meals that you're likely to find anywhere," notes NLC partner John Howard whose castle-like home on Tintern Road is opposite the site.

"Nowhere else in the world have great chefs found such diversity and high food quality than here in Niagara – yet we take it all for granted," adds Howard who is also owner of an entirely separate business, the Vineland Estates winery, vineyards and restaurant near the NLC site.

> "We grow some of the best fruit and vegetables, some of the best materials for great meals that you're likely to find anywhere… Nowhere else in the world have great chefs found such diversity and high food quality - yet we take it for granted."

Howard and NLC partner Paul Mazza, a Hamilton lawyer, have taken on a larger position in NLC after buying out former partners.

"We're establishing a place that's designed to profile all of the essential elements of a Niagara food and wine experience," Howard explains.

"You'll be able to stay overnight after sampling wines," he adds.

"If you want to gain a hands-on experience of what it's all about, you can work in the vineyard, the winery or the kitchen," Howard notes.

"You can also help source food for the centre's restaurant. You can attend cooking demonstrations or get the lesson on television in your room."

Howard says the centre will foster a better understanding of Niagara's food and wine industries.

"We want to give the consumer the opportunity to gain a full appreciation of the culinary experience that's grown up around the wines," he explains.

"World-class chefs tell us how strong our source material is. Now visitors will have a chance to experience the foods and wines that are here. People should understand how fortunate they are to live in - or visit - this country."

The New World Culinary Centre will preserve area farmland by creating a market for surrounding vineyards and local produce, Howard notes.

"It will allow people with farms as small as 20 acres to plant more exotic legumes and receive a better return for their efforts," he explains.

"Having more vibrant, successful farms around us will also give us something of a buffer around our vineyards," he adds.

"It will help prevent urbanization as the farmlands will provide their owners with a reasonable return so they won't want to sell their land to developers. We may even see an expansion of vineyards and agricultural land use"

The win-win situation doesn't end there: More than 100 jobs are to be created by the New World Culinary Centre. It will also play a role in attracting investment to Niagara region and strengthen the local economy.

The centre will also feature the expertise of its director, Mark Picone whose culinary magic is already familiar to patrons of Vineland Estates where he serves as executive chef.

Howard is clearly proud of the centre: "More than anything else, the centre will promote an awareness of the unique agricultural character of the Niagara region and our tremendous potential in agriculture and tourism."

➤ *John Howard and the Niagara Land Company are fostering an appreciation of area wines and food.*

Overleaf: John Howard's home.

Niagara Land Company

- *Photo by Paul Sparrow*

Enterprise 2000

Enterprise 2000

HAMILTON
Hub of the Golden Horseshoe

Dawn. A new day's light softly illuminates office complexes and high-rise apartment towers defining Hamilton's skyline.

The city's famous steel mills fall under the strengthening morning light. Further west, Hamilton's industrial harbourfront gives way to parkland. The sun shimmers on calm recreational waters as sailboat enthusiasts greet the new day.

Behind the city skyline, past lower city parks and neighbourhoods, a stretch of the Niagara Escarpment emerges from shadow, its steep sides and rocky cliffs reminding everyone why this section of escarpment is better known as Hamilton Mountain.

Visitors to Hamilton are often struck by how attractive the city is. Its vistas, parks and pleasant neighbourhoods can quickly dispel any lingering, outdated images of Hamilton as a gritty centre of heavy industry.

Yet, the city is also proud of its heavy industrial heritage, prouder still that it remains home to many heavy and light industries. And Canada's Steel City is more than a little proud that it's home to the nation's two largest steelmakers, Stelco Inc. and Dofasco Inc. Many millions of dollars in technology investments have made the steel giants efficient, high tech companies that produce more tons of steel per man-hour than most of their rivals in Canada, the United States and Europe.

Yet, while the steel industry and support industries remain a major source of employment in Hamilton, the city's economy has steadily diversified over the years. The health care services sector now employs more people in Hamilton than any other sector.

And this is one of the most livable cities in the world. It boasts an abundance of parks, numerous festivals, a recreational waterfront, relatively little traffic congestion, less pollution than many other major cities, low unemployment, affordable housing and an overall quality of life that is the envy of many communities.

The city is also a major centre of commerce and has seen a proliferation of shopping malls and 'box' stores spring up in recent decades within the city proper and its suburban communities, which include Ancaster, Dundas, Flamborough, Glanbrook and Stoney Creek.

With Hamilton itself, they comprise Hamilton-Wentworth region, a regional municipality with a population approaching half a million people. Burlington and Grimsby are also often included as part of Greater Hamilton.

By the late 1990s, the population of Hamilton-Wentworth approached 470,000 people – more than 320,000 of them residing in Hamilton itself.

Add in the interdependent and interconnected regions of Halton and Niagara and it's apparent Hamilton is the economic and geographic hub of a sprawling, diversified economic region that is home to more than one million people.

Hamilton: Hub of the Golden Horseshoe

Picture-perfect Gore Park, a downtown oasis.

- Photo by Paul Sparrow

The borders of this vast economic region are also somewhat elastic and can include Haldimand-Norfolk lands to the south, Grimsby to the east and Brant County to the west, increasing the population to over 1.2 million.

It's a Hamilton-centred hinterland of shared geography and economic interests. And this economic region boasts a highly diversified economy, including everything from soft fruit growing and winemaking, to heavy industry and high tech companies.

Nick Catalano, economic development director for Hamilton-Wentworth region, is at the forefront of efforts to help Greater Hamilton realize its rich potential.

Catalano is focusing on how Hamilton can best take advantage of its enviable position at the hub of one of North America's most densely populated international markets. Within a 500-mile radius of Hamilton, about a day's drive, is a total market population of 120 million people.

"We're successfully getting the message out that, as proud as we are of our steel industry, there's a whole lot more to Hamilton than steel," Catalano asserts in an informative interview at his downtown Hamilton offices.

Catalano notes international business ties are being developed through the Bordernet organization promoting importing and exporting with the U.S.

"Hamilton companies now export more than 50 per cent of the goods and services produced in this city," he states with pride. "Most of these exports are to the United States. There's a tremendous about of cross border trade that takes place here."

Indeed, Hamilton is also a major distribution centre with one of the nation's busiest harbours. U.S. Air at Hamilton Airport continues to service the city's international air traffic needs and the airport is today a major hub for cargo/courier services. Hamilton's international connections appear destined to continue growing in years, decades and centuries to come.

Catalano also points to emerging opportunities within Hamilton itself.

Brownfields, vacated or underused lands that once housed industries, are giving rise to new companies and new sources of employment, he notes.

One of the most striking examples of a virtual brownfield being transformed into a bustling centre of commerce can be found on Hamilton's industrialized waterfront.

An entire community of small businesses has now found a home in

The golden glow of Hamilton, a city rich with opportunity.

- Photo by Paul Sparrow

Hamilton: Hub of the Golden Horseshoe

Hamilton: The Ambitious City by the Bay.

Hamilton: Hub of the Golden Horseshoe

- Photo by Paul Sparrow

old, previously vacated factories and warehouses that once were used by industrial giants.

This industrial park space is now being leased by the Hamilton Harbour Commissioners at low rental rates to an array of tenants, including De Feo's Auto Service Ltd.

Owner Sergio De Feo has steadily expanded his business, establishing several service bays in a former industrial warehouse. De Feo's, at the foot of Hillyard Street, has become a favoured location for expert auto repairs at reasonable rates.

Numerous other businesses have made their home in the immediate area, including McKeil Marine and Heddle Marine. Both firms are given profile treatment later in this chapter.

The new, information age, economy is also bringing new job opportunities. Montreal-based Media Express has set up a Hamilton fibre optic call centre operation at Lloyd D. Jackson Square, creating 450 jobs.

Catalano notes efforts are underway to develop Hamilton's 'smart community' potential, via uplinks to satellite linkages, allowing doctors many miles apart to have a fibre optic consultation on television screens. A diagnosis or patient information can be shared instantly via multimedia, telecommunication uplink technology.

John Dolbec, executive director of the Hamilton & District Chamber of Commerce, notes two other firms, Cogeco and Union Energy, are joining Media Express in establishing call centres in Hamilton.

"Altogether, between the three companies, we're looking at something in order of 900 jobs," Dolbec smiles in an interview at the Hamilton & District Chamber of Commerce office.

"That level of job growth is impressive," Dolbec adds. "It means that even with the lose of hundreds at Procter & Gamble, M.A. Henry and J.I. Case, we still have a net gain of jobs from call centres alone."

That such dynamic endeavours

Hamilton: Hub of the Golden Horseshoe

The Hess Village Jazz Festival - just one of Hamilton's many concert attractions.

Enterprise 2000

Hamilton: Hub of the Golden Horseshoe

would locate in downtown Hamilton shouldn't be surprising. The city's core boasts an abundance of available space at relatively low rates.

Although still struggling in places, Hamilton's downtown is seeing many millions of dollars in investment, including the renovated John Sopinka court house, renovations to the old Spectator building, street improvements and the development of downtown condominium buildings.

The Royal Connaught Howard Johnson Plaza Hotel has also undergone millions of dollars worth of renovations and the Sheraton Hamilton is playing a vital economic role in revitalizing the downtown core. Both hotels are profiled later in this chapter and further information on these and other companies can be obtained by calling the telephone numbers listed in the directory at the back of this book.

"Hamilton's downtown will eventually reinvigorate itself," Catalano suggests, "because it offers reasonable lease rates, it's a destination location for entertainment and its economy continues to diversify."

"There are phenomenal opportunities downtown," he adds. "The realty prices are low, the problems are solvable and the potential is great."

Catalano also notes the city's entire economy has diversified. After years of downsizing, the big industries seem to have found an employment balance and they remain a secure source of existing jobs. The Manufacturing sector is vibrant, the health care and education sectors are growing and the entire services sector is expanding.

Hamilton's unemployment rate – just 4.2 per cent in the summer of 1999 – is often the lowest in Canada. Labour force participation rates are growing and the local economy generated 13,000 new jobs in the first few months of 1999 alone.

"We're certainly doing everything possible to foster the image that Hamilton is a good community to invest in," says Catalano. "We have the

Hamilton: Hub of the Golden Horseshoe

A highrise view of Hamilton's bustling downtown core.

Hamilton: Hub of the Golden Horseshoe

- Photo by Paul Sparrow

lowest unemployment rates anywhere, a highly skilled labour force, a great quality of life and, compared to many other centres, the cost of doing business here is low. We also offer fast, convenient access to other markets in Toronto and the U.S."

To Catalano, Hamilton offers all of the amenities of a major city without many of the often-attendant problems of congestion and stress.

"In every area you can possible think of, Hamilton continues to provide an enviable place to live, work and play."

Catalano also observes that the community has become a well-organized whole with once-distant institutions regularly conferring with each other to devise programs that can best exploit the new commercial and employment opportunities a changing business world is offering.

His own department is in regular contact with the Hamilton & District Chamber of Commerce, Mohawk College, McMaster University and the Greater Hamilton Technology Enterprise Centre (GHTEC) which is 98 per cent leased and serves as an incubator for start-up high-tech firms.

"It's a terrific alliance - there are no turf wars anymore," Catalano proudly states, "just a common desire to work together to solve our problems and help our community prosper."

Lee Kirkby, a former executive director at the chamber, agrees.

"There's a strong sense of everyone working together to face common challenges – you don't find that in very many communities."

Dolbec, the 1999 executive director, concurs and stresses the importance of matching job skills with job needs.

"We're frequently faced with shortages of skilled labour," Dolbec notes. "Anyone with marketable skills like tool and die makers, electricians, carpenters and machinists is finding it relatively easy to find work," he says.

Dolbec notes many skilled trades people are middle-aged or older and there is no new generation of skilled

Hamilton: Hub of the Golden Horseshoe

The Davie family enjoys a visit to Sam Lawrence Park overlooking Hamilton's skyline.

- Photo by Paul Sparrow

trades to replace this aging workforce.

"The demand for new skilled trades people is there – the supply isn't. It's important that we find ways, develop programs, to create the skills that are needed in our community."

Dolbec notes Ontario Flightcraft could have expanded but it was unable to take on more orders because the company needed 45 to 50 skilled people and couldn't find them.

"It's unfortunate some firms lose business because they lack skilled trades people and can't find them."

Dolbec says the Ontario-wide shortage of skilled trades presents a huge opportunity for those people willing to learn a trade.

"Unfortunately, not many young people are interested. There seems to be a stigma about working with your

hands even if you're paid $50,000."

"Business hasn't done enough to train future generations and it's coming back to haunt us," he adds.

"However, there are genuine efforts underway to address this problem. Businesses are working closely with community colleges to create and promote programs to create the skills."

Dolbec takes heart in the work being done to ensure a new generation has the option of going into a trade.

"There's more of a willingness and effort to address these problems than there perhaps has been in some time."

Catalano likes the community spirit he's encountering. "The general mood in this community is one of confidence and optimism," Catalano asserts. "With all the downsizing and upheaval that has occurred everywhere, Hamilton has

emerged with a stronger, more diversified economy. We're in a good position to take on any challenges the new millennium may bring."

Dolbec says Hamilton's favorable position is owed in part to it geographical location in the huge Southern Ontario market with access to the even greater U.S. market.

He says the Canada-U.S. Free Trade Agreement and North American Free Trade Agreement have succeeded in giving Hamilton companies unfettered access to the American market.

"There were concerns from some that free trade would cost jobs. What we've found instead is that free trade has saved jobs and created jobs."

Dolbec observes that one of the primary beneficiaries of the FTA has been Hamilton's manufacturing sector.

Hamilton: Hub of the Golden Horseshoe

"Hamilton still has a very strong manufacturing sector," he notes. "Manufacturing is still the leading source of existing jobs and new jobs."

But the service sector is experience phenomenal growth, he adds.

"Services oriented companies have gone from accounting for 34 per cent of the chamber's membership to 50 per cent in the past four years while manufacturing members account for 16 per cent," he notes. "Yet manufacturing overall is still the leading source of all jobs."

"That may sound surprising," Dolbec admits, "because Stelco and Dofasco only employ half the number of people they employed in the early 1980s. But a lot of the new jobs are coming from new manufacturers."

"For example," he explains, "Décor Pre-cast, which makes patio stones, has gone from 40 employees to 130 and its sales to the U.S. have quintupled in past four to five years."

Dolbec asserts that most of the growth in manufacturing jobs has occurred outside the steel industry via an abundance of small manufacturers each employing less than 100 people.

"We also have growth in high tech and information services," he adds.

"And entrepreneurs are creating many of these new jobs. People getting into business on their own are creating their own job plus additional jobs for other people."

The chamber has 2,700 members, of which 1,100 are companies and 1,600 are individuals. Small businesses, including home-based businesses, now constitute the fastest growing source of members at the chamber and this has led the organization to devote more time and energy representing the concerns of small business.

That change in approach reflects a societal reality: Small businesses dominate the new age economy.

Dolbec observes that small business remains the primary source of new jobs "and that's probably a good thing. It would seem to be healthier to

depend on many small companies for jobs than rely on one or two big firms to create employment."

He says that with growing numbers of entrepreneurs and small businesses starting up and thriving, the economy is becoming more and more diverse.

"Diversity is a real strength. You're not as dependent on one or two sectors of the economy or one or two companies to keep you going. Economic changes that hurt some companies may not hurt others. Having a diversified economy means you're in a better position to withstand an inevitable recession."

Dolbec says diversity is just one of the competitive advantages enjoyed by the Greater Hamilton area.

"Another strength is the ability of many of our companies to make specialized products and services for niche markets," he notes.

"We also benefit from a low-valued dollar which helps our exports compete abroad, our low real estate costs, and our lower costs of doing business," he adds.

"When you look at all of our strengths, it's apparent that our economy is healthier now than perhaps it's ever been. We seem to be in good shape going into the new millennium."

For researchers or anyone interested

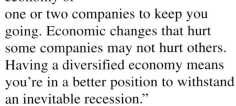

Diane Sonego doesn't need glasses.   *- Photo by Paul Sparrow*

in acquiring more information on some of the firms, agencies, organizations and individuals cited throughout this book, turn to the Enterprise 2000 directory at the back of the book and call the firms for further details.

Meanwhile, in the profile stories just ahead, you'll learn more about McKeil Marine and Heddle Marine.

You'll also gain an appreciation of the economic contribution made to Hamilton's downtown core by its major hotels: the Sheraton Hamilton Hotel and the Royal Connaught Howard Johnson Plaza Hotel.

And you can expect to come away inspired after reading the story of Jody Bertozzi and DOVE Marketing.

Finally, you'll learn about a new Hamilton Laser Eye Institute vision treatment – and find out what Diane Sonego, pictured above, is doing with a pile of discarded glasses.

You'll find all this and more, next.

Hamilton Laser Eye Institute

Diane Sonego was legally blind when she finally opted for laser eye surgery. A few hours later, she had nearly perfect vision.

"It was just amazing," Sonego recollects of the 1997 operation. "I had the surgery, went home and dozed off on the couch. When I woke up, I glanced at the TV and I could see the picture clearly without wearing glasses or contact lenses."

Sonego found the LASIK surgical procedure was a liberating experience.

"The next day I drove my car – and left the glasses and contact lenses at home," she recalls with a smile.

"Now I can't imagine what life was like wearing contacts – even though the operation was just a couple years ago," she adds, still very much in awe of the profound impact of the surgery.

"It was wonderful," Sonego exclaims in an interview at Hamilton Laser Eye Institute offices on Upper Wentworth Street at Mohawk Road in Hamilton where she serves as manager and director of marketing.

Sonego, 35, has also enjoyed a long-standing professional relationship with the Windsor Laser Eye Institute head office. She had joined the parent firm in 1981 as an ophthalmic technician.

"The biggest obstacles people have to overcome are apprehension about the operation and the cost," Sonego points out, drawing on her own experience and that of other patients.

"I had the opportunity, over many years, to have this done," she admits, "but I had to get past my own feelings of fear and anxiety even though I know the doctors are excellent."

During the LASIK refractive surgery, the patient remains awake but their eyes are frozen with drops. A small flap is created on the epithelial layer of the cornea and lifted back. A computer assisted laser device applies just the right amount of Exemer Laser energy to the cornea beneath the flap to correct the refractive error. The flap is then placed back on the eye and the eye heals within 24 hours.

The entire procedure takes all of two minutes per eye. It captures 70 to 80 per cent of previously missing vision almost immediately. Remaining vision is obtained within a day.

Although painkillers are sometimes prescribed after surgery, Sonego, like many patients, found she didn't need any. After spending less than five minutes in the operating room, the glasses and contact lenses she'd worn since high school were history. She now chides herself for waiting so long.

> "It's great to see the change it makes in people's lives, to see how pleased the patients are that they can read a paper or an alarm clock without having to wear glasses."

"I assisted in the operation room and I had seen a lot of procedures done without problems," she recalls. "But I was nervous – I guess you're always a little apprehensive about eye surgery."

Dr. Fouad Tayfour, the first surgeon in North America to perform refractive laser eye surgery, founded the Windsor Laser Eye Institute in 1981. He also presides over a Michigan clinic and the Hamilton institute that began in 1997 at Limeridge Medical Centre.

By the spring of 1999, the Hamilton Laser Eye Institute had outgrown the centre and moved to much larger quarters at its current location where 1,500 laser eye surgeries are performed annually, up from 200 in 1997.

Medical director Dr. Lawrence Kobetz, a cataract surgeon, heads the institute's ophthalmology team. The other team members are: Drs. Jeffrey

Sher, a corneal surgeon; Vineet Arora, a retinal surgeon; and John Harvey, an oculoplastics (eyelids) surgeon. All four doctors have worked at other laser eye centres and practice in Hamilton.

Arora notes the surgery corrects many problems of near-sightedness, far-sightedness or astigmatism, steepening or flattening the curvature of the eye by reshaping the cornea.

"It's great to see the change it makes in people's lives, to see how pleased the patients are that they can read a paper or an alarm clock without having to wear glasses."

Kobetz notes the computer software is continually updated to keep surgical procedures literally on the cutting edge.

"We're getting to the point where we can pretty well reshape tissue into anything we want," he proudly states.

Not everyone is a candidate for laser eye surgery. For example, Harvey continues to wear glasses because his cornea is irregularly shaped.

But he has complete faith in the procedure for those patients whose free eye test shows they're good candidates.

"The chance of a person actually having a poor outcome is very, very small," he notes.

Sher also has complete faith in the procedure: "I'm confident enough in the LASIK surgery to have had it done on my own eyes," he says with pride.

"Most patients are absolutely thrilled," he notes. "They have 70-80 per cent of vision back immediately."

Former patients happily corroborate.

An athlete, who felt limited in sports by glasses and contact lenses, recalls being "just ecstatic," after the surgery.

A severely near-sighted woman, who wore glasses for 35 years, now has 20/20 vision after LASKIK surgery.

"It was," she asserts, "the best investment I ever made."

➢ *Drs. Lawrence Kobetz, Jeffrey Sher, Vineet Arora and John Harvey have a clear vision of the challenges ahead.*

Hamilton Laser Eye Institute

- Photo by Michael Dismatsek

Enterprise 2000

McKeil Marine

It's the most extraordinary service McKeil Marine has ever provided.

In the remote city of Maceio on Brazil's east coast, impoverished children rush towards a smiling Blair McKeil, president of the Hamilton marine services company.

The children embrace McKeil, then walk with him to his destination: an orphanage, funded by McKeil Marine.

Once inside the compound, McKeil briefs resident caregivers on his plans to move the orphanage to a larger home and install a soccer field, orchards and a swimming pool to serve around 20 parentless youngsters.

McKeil's orphanage already provides food, shelter, dental, medical and educational services to the orphans. It also runs a soup kitchen, providing meals to many neighbouring families.

Back home in Hamilton, McKeil agrees that few people know of his orphanage or the story behind it.

And it's an inspiring story.

In the mid 1990s, McKeil and his wife Lois adopted newborn twin boys from Maceio, Brazil.

"While we were going through the adoption process with our own sons, Wyatt and Jarrett, we became aware of the ongoing hardships of the other children living there," McKeil recalls.

"We wanted to do something to improve their lives," he adds, in an interview at McKeil Marine's head office on Hamilton's waterfront.

"Many children were abandoned. Some didn't know who their birth parents were. We assisted an existing orphanage that was about to close due to lack of funds, and expanded it."

McKeil keeps in touch with the orphanage and continues to play the lead role in its expansion.

This little-known charitable effort is having a remarkable impact on the children of this Brazilian city and on the many Canadians, Americans and Europeans who adopt the youngsters.

McKeil's charitable work is one side of a multifaceted businessman whose imaginative approach doesn't end with transforming an orphanage.

In mid-July, McKeil Marine went out to retrieve two B17 bombers that had landed on an ice flow off the coast of Greenland during the Second World War. Although the bomber's crew was rescued, the plane sank in frigid waters weeks later as the war overseas raged.

> "While we were going through the adoption process with our own sons, Wyatt and Jarrett, we became aware of the ongoing hardships of the other children living there… We wanted to do something to improve their lives."

Half a century later, McKeil Marine is on hire to retrieve the bombers from depths exceeding 800 feet as part of the Greenland Memorial Expedition attended by survivors of the wartime crash. National Geographic and The Discovery Channel are also involved. The bombers will be refurbished for display in an aviation museum.

Around the same time, another of McKeil's tug boats was en route to Chile while other tugs and barges went to jobs in Puerto Rico and Ungava Bay in Canada's sub Arctic.

A McKeil Marine crew recently went 95 days without seeing land while towing two barges from where they had been purchased in Singapore to their new owner in Mexico.

In the late 1990s, McKeil Marine acquired a number of smaller companies serving niche markets in ship docking, towing, and service to the oil and gas sectors.

The McKeil Marine group consists of six operating firms Great Lakes, the St. Lawrence Seaway, and the Eastern Seaboard and venturing to the Canadian sub Arctic, the Gulf of Mexico, and beyond.

This group now boasts a fleet well in excess of 100 tugs and barges. The firm employs more than 150 people, with its head office on Hillyard Street.

It's all part of a journey that began more than 40 years ago when Blair McKeil's father, Evans McKeil, founded the Hamilton-based company.

For Evans McKeil, the business was in his blood. As a child in Pugwash, N.S., in the 1930s, he watched his uncles sail cargo-laden schooners.

After the Second World War, a teenaged Evans McKeil helped his father William McKeil, a lumber mill owner; build boats. So it's not surprising this transplanted blue-noser is today chairman of McKeil Marine, operating the largest tugboat and barge fleet on the Great Lakes.

In 1949, a languishing Maritime economy convinced Evans McKeil to go to Hamilton. He joined the former McNamara Marine in 1950, dredging and building bridges and docks.

In 1956, at the suggestion of a Newfoundland skipper, Evans McKeil ventured out on his own, built the MicMac, a 35-foot-long workboat, and McKeil Marine was born. His brother Doug McKeil joined in the early 1960s and fixed boats bought from the Royal Canadian Navy and other sources.

The company is truly a family affair with Evans McKeil, his brother Doug, sons Blair and Garth, as well as numerous other family members playing various roles in the business.

Blair McKeil was named president in 1992 and became responsible for overseeing company operations. Under his leadership, the firm has achieved steady growth. But he's quick to credit employees for the firm's success.

"The main contributing factor to our success is our people."

> ➤ *Flanked by sons Wyatt and Jarrett, Blair McKeil continues to steer McKeil Marine towards growth .*

McKeil Marine

Enterprise 2000

Heddle Marine

Just 10 years after starting out as a tiny firm, Heddle Marine Service is set to begin repairing the biggest freighters plying the waters of the Great Lakes and St. Lawrence River.

To expand into the market for large vessel repairs, Heddle Marine plans to build a third floating dry dock at its sprawling Hamilton Harbour site.

The new floating dry dock will allow the Hamilton boat repair company to paint and repair 730-foot-long Great Lakes freighters, the largest vessels currently allowed in the Great Lakes.

This move also places the firm on the threshold of increased, sustainable growth and enhanced profitability.

"There's a lot more we can do once we can dock the larger vessels," explains Heddle Marine President Richard Heddle in an interview at his office at the foot of Hillyard Street.

"It's an opportunity that will allow us to continue to grow in this market," adds Heddle, 34, who is pleased and excited concerning the business challenges that lie ahead.

He anticipates the added business from the large vessel market will accelerate his company's growth, allowing it to gradually expand its workforce from its late-1990s level of 40 people to some 60-80 people early in the new millennium.

The move to large vessel repairs is a major stage in the evolution of this innovative company that traces its origins to a one-man proprietorship in 1987. The firm incorporated as Heddle Marine Service Inc. in 1989.

"Back in 1987, the company was just myself and one employee," Heddle recalls with a smile. "In 1989 there was four or five of us and we've continued to grow from there."

Although born and raised in the rural Stoney Creek farming community of Winona, Heddle actually grew up around boats.

His neighbours included the McKeil family of McKeil Marine, the marine services firm next to his current site.

"During my childhood I could often be found visiting their facilities in Hamilton," Heddle recalls, "and I also went down to Port Dover quite often to check out the boats on Lake Erie. Even though our home was on Highway 8, I spent so much time around boats, I basically grew up on the water."

"There's a lot more we can do once we can dock the larger vessels… It's an opportunity that will allow us to continue to grow in this market."

Even as a youngster, Heddle was mechanically inclined and his youthful hands could regularly be found taking apart lawn mowers and bikes.

At age 15, he worked a summer in the maintenance shop at E.D. Smith.

He also worked a co-op term with National Machinery in Winona, doing machining and repair work. He served a millwright apprenticeship there and went into partnership with the firm's owner, Herbert Ruzika.

This partnership jointly invented and patented a mechanism for the operating of valves involved in the running of large heating and air conditioning units. Their company was later sold to a larger firm, which acquired rights to this device. Some of the proceeds from this sale, plus an investment by the McKeil family, would later finance Heddle Marine.

"Those early years were a great learning experience," Heddle recalls with enthusiasm.

"Just getting involved in many things at a young age and applying the knowledge I gained, helped me a lot when it came to going into business on my own later on," adds Heddle who is both a certified millwright and a certified hoisting engineer.

The company initially performed only 'top-side' repairs and painting work to the portion of boats above the waterline. Then, in 1990, the company completed construction of its first floating dry dock at Pier 15 in Hamilton Harbour. The 250-foot long, 3,200-tonne-capacity dry dock can dock boats up to 400-feet long.

This floating dry dock was moved westward to Heddle Marine's current, much larger location at Pier 14.

A second floating dry dock, 325-feet long with a 6,500-tonne capacity, began construction in 1997. Two barges were salvaged to form the base of this dry dock completed in 1998.

A third floating dry dock, the same size as the second is now in the planning stage and would allow the firm to begin repairing the largest lake freighters allowed on the Great Lakes.

Situated on land leased from the Hamilton Harbour Commissioners, the Heddle marine site boasts 160,000-square-feet of land, 1,000 feet of wharfage and dock frontage and about 1,000-square-feet of office space, plus the dry docks and 5,000-square-feet of shop space. About 10-25 vessels are repaired each year from this location.

The company's largest job involved using the first and second dry docks together to dock a 630-foot-long freighter. The stern was then cut off and removed in preparation for a new stern for the 7,500-tonne vessel.

For jobs big or small, Heddle knows he can count on his well-trained staff.

"It's the people here that make the company successful," he asserts.

"I'm fortunate to have some very dedicated people working here."

➤ *Richard Heddle is set to pursue new opportunities at Heddle Marine Service Inc.*

Heddle Marine

- Photo by Paul Sparrow

Enterprise 2000

Dove Marketing

"We've worked so hard for this - and now it's happened!" an excited Jody Bertozzi exclaims as he hangs up the phone.

Bertozzi, president of DOVE Marketing and Promotions, quickly apologizes for interrupting our interview, then rushes off to share the news with his staff of 12.

The News? A Canadian Automobile Association national advertising and promotions contract worth hundreds of thousands of dollars has just been awarded to Hamilton-based DOVE.

A moment later Bertozzi is back.

"I had to let our staff know about this," explains Bertozzi, 38. "They've burned the midnight oil every night for weeks working on this."

Nodding in agreement, his partner in business and life Kristen Fralick, 29, observes "the staff have worked very hard to make this business self-supporting."

Wide smiles are now shared by the young couple who met in 1996 at Mohawk College where she works as a certified general accountant and financial officer for the Mohawk College Students Association.

"We've come a long way since starting this company as an idea in the basement of my townhouse," says Bertozzi, a Mohawk Advertising graduate who served as president of the student council and is now a director of the alumni association.

"This is a real turning point."

It's also the latest step in Bertozzi's own evolution into a dynamic marketer with an inspiring story of loss and achievement.

Asked how he became so involved in marketing, Bertozzi replies dryly that he "fell into it."

The comment can be taken literally.

On October 3, 1990, Bertozzi was fixing a school roof when he became distracted, stepped off the edge and fell four storeys to pavement below.

Until that moment, it had been a routine day for Bertozzi, a partner in Bertozzi Roofing, the family firm he'd worked at since childhood with his father Julian and brother Tim.

The fall shattered his life.

Two weeks later, Bertozzi awoke from the blackness of a coma to experience his first epileptic seizure.

Doctors told him he had sustained brain damage and a broken back. They said he would never walk again and would forever be plagued by epilepsy.

> "They told me I'd never walk again and I'd have epileptic seizures for life. But I walk perfectly now – and I haven't had a seizure since 1997. I thank God the doctors were wrong."

Bertozzi was advised to have back surgery although there was only a slim chance of any recovery. He was also given epilepsy medication "that made me feel numb, like a zombie."

Even with the medication, Bertozzi suffered weekly epileptic seizures.

By 1993, he'd had enough. He turned down back surgery and went off his epilepsy medication.

Bertozzi turned instead to his wife Sandy, a homeopath who prescribed natural treatments of herbal medicines.

Within months, Bertozzi was walking and functioning again.

"They told me I'd never walk again and I'd have epileptic seizures for life," Bertozzi recalls. "But I walk perfectly now – and I haven't had a seizure since 1997. I thank God the doctors were wrong."

While recovering, Bertozzi knew his broken body couldn't handle the physical demands of roofing.

He began to consider alternatives, especially marketing. "Even when I was roofing," he recalls, "I worked on our advertising. I enjoyed doing that."

By late 1993, Bertozzi was feeling well enough to perform work that was not physically demanding. He began marketing and promotional work for Labatt Breweries. He also became a continuing education student at Mohawk, studying Advertising.

Bertozzi took 1995 off to care for his wife Sandy who was dying of cancer.

In 1996, Bertozzi completed his Advertising program and left Labatt, determined to start up his own firm.

With borrowed money from family and Kristen's parents, his own savings and a $29,000 bank loan, Bertozzi invested $100,000 to start DOVE marketing, named for doves he keeps in his office as symbols of peace.

"We really started on a shoestring budget," Bertozzi recalls. "But we're grateful for the support we received from family and from Peter Dyer, the head of Media Studies at Mohawk, who helped us with the logistics.

In two years, the firm had amassed $1 million in sales.

The full-service firm does everything from media buying and graphic design to event planning, website design, marketing plans and in-house printing from spacious offices in an industrial building on Wentworth Street North.

Bertozzi, a lifelong Hamiltonian, believes much more can be done with the city's industrial properties. He intends to run for mayor in the fall of 2000 to put into motion his vision and action plan for revitalizing Hamilton.

And he'll continue to run DOVE, providing clients with tailor-made marketing solutions with no payment expected if results are not satisfactory.

"So far," Bertozzi notes, "everyone has been happy and we've been paid."

"Our client list is growing from referrals. Our people do great work and we provide measurable results."

> ➢ *Jody Bertozzi and Kristen Fralick are pleased with DOVE's Marketing success.*

Dove Marketing

- Photo by Paul Sparrow

Enterprise 2000

Sheraton Hamilton Hotel

The Sheraton Hamilton Hotel's importance to Hamilton's downtown goes beyond presenting a polished, welcoming image of the city to guests from around the world.

The prestigious, four-diamond, five-star hotel is also one of downtown Hamilton's largest employers, directly accounting for 250 full-time and part-time jobs plus dozens of indirect spin-off jobs at firms servicing the hotel.

As well, several dozen people are employed at 14 neighboring mall stores owned by the hotel, which adjoins Lloyd D. Jackson Square.

And the Sheraton Hamilton Hotel's positive economic impact doesn't end there: It serves as the 'headquarters' hotel for numerous special events and conventions that bring many millions of dollars in spending and investment into the city every year.

It's also a favoured place to stay for a lengthy list of the rich and famous, including Bob Hope, Tom Jones, Garth Brooks and Wayne Gretzky.

Political guest luminaries include Canadian prime ministers Jean Chretien, Brian Mulroney, John Turner and Joe Clark, U.S. presidents George Bush and Gerald Ford and former British PM Margaret Thatcher.

Beyond continually putting Hamilton in the spotlight and acting as a magnet for investment, the Sheraton Hamilton Hotel also supports numerous local causes, including the sponsoring of Theatre Aquarius, Opera Hamilton, The CFL Hamilton Tiger-Cats and Hamilton Symphony Orchestra. The Hamilton landmark hotel also hosts an annual Labour Day Telethon and it hosts a 'Home For The Holidays' event every Christmas in which the hotel works with local hospital to provide free hotel rooms for families of terminally ill patients for up to a week's stay.

"We try to be a valuable part of Hamilton and to give back to this community as much as we can," notes Jim Awad, 48, general manager of the Sheraton Hamilton Hotel since 1988.

"We like to be an active supporter of as many community events as we possibly can," adds Awad, who is also vice-president of operations for the North American division of GGS Hotel Holdings Canada Inc.

> "We try to be a valuable part of Hamilton and to give back to this community as much as we can… We like to be an active supporter of … many community events…"

Awad, as a GGS vice-president, is responsible for the $50-million US profitable operation of the 1600 rooms at nine North American hotels, including the Sheraton Hamilton.

And he clearly enjoys his dual role as GM of the Hamilton landmark, taking pride in the hotel's progress.

"Our occupancy has gone from 53 per cent of our rooms to 70 per cent and our average daily rate has increased to $100 in the past ten years," Awad notes, attributing part of the gain to the hotel staff's readiness to respond to customer input.

Based on the comments of guests, the hotel is providing a décor that is homier while retaining an understated sense of elegance. Many rooms also contain fax machines and computer hookups in keeping with Awad's strategy to build corporate clientele.

"We're looking more and more into ways we can make our hotel as user-friendly as possible,' Awad explains.

The hotel also prides itself on its creative and innovative spirit. To bring in the new millennium, the Sheraton Hamilton planned a New Year's Eve event like no other.

The all-inclusive 1-2 day Voyage 2000 event meant transforming the hotel into a virtual ship. Guests boarded the hotel and checked into their 'cabins' before exploring rooms offering tastes of ancient Egyptian, Roman and Greek civilizations. After various events, guests entered 2000 in a futuristic room with laser light show.

The impressive, 18-storey hotel features 300 rooms and suites, including the very-spacious Hamilton Suite and the Prime Minister's Suite. These super suites are among those to be found on the hotel's top three floors, known as the Club levels.

The hotel features a swimming pool, sauna, Jacuzzi, exercise room, meeting rooms and restaurants, plus access to stores in Jackson Square and passage to the Hamilton Convention Centre, Copps Coliseum and the Ronald V. Joyce Centre for the Performing Arts at Hamilton Place.

"We have a lot to offer in the way of amenities," Awad agrees with a smile.

"But our main asset is not the building, it's not the bricks and mortar - it's the people we work with and the people we host here every day."

Awad explains that staff operates by a code of honour and ethics emphasizing trust, reliability honesty and teamwork. This is combined with a sense of ownership; desire to please clients and commitment to excellence.

"All of this forms the foundation from which we can offer the best service possible," Awad notes.

"We need, at all times, to make our guests happy, excited and satisfied that they've experienced the best this hotel has to offer."

> ➢ *Jim Awad invites guests to experience the very best the Sheraton Hamilton offers.*

Sheraton Hamilton Hotel

- Photo by Paul Sparrow

Enterprise 2000

Royal Connaught Howard Johnson Hotel

Dubbed the 'Grand Old Lady of Hamilton', The Royal Connaught Howard Johnson Plaza Hotel is a treasured Hamilton landmark.

With its understated elegance and stately charm, the venerable hotel remains one of Canada's finest facilities. It offers comfortable overnight accommodations, space for meetings and conventions, and various on-site attractions including a Yuk Yuk's Comedy Club venue.

Officially opened more than 85 years ago by the Duke of Connaught, the venerable hotel has played host to an array of notable guests, including Prime Minister Lester B. Pearson, Ontario Premier Mike Harris, country music stars Shania Twain and Michelle Wright and comedian Martin Short.

Pierre Trudeau and former wife Margaret were also among the many well-known guests to enjoy a quiet escape from the public eye in the comfortable confines of the hotel.

"It's still the Grand Old Lady of Hamilton and it's truly one of Canada's great hotels," notes hotel manager Louis Jaketic, who is emphasizing the old and new at this landmark establishment that overlooks Gore Park in the heart of downtown.

The Connaught has gone through a number of improvements in recent years and its elegant ballroom lobby evokes a sense of nostalgia and luxury as guests commemorate the hotel's central role in Hamilton's social life.

In addition to Old World charm, it has such modern features as an indoor swimming pool and giant water slide.

Popular in-hotel attractions feature restaurant and bar facilities, and, of course, Yuk Yuk's comedy club. There are also other businesses, including travel agents and a gift shop.

The hotel offers seasonal family packages featuring price discounts and free accommodations for children under age 18 sharing a room with their parents. The packages are a terrific bargain, both for visitors to Hamilton

The Royal Connaught Howard Johnson Plaza Hotel.   *- Photo by Paul Sparrow*

and for native Hamiltonians looking for an enjoyable nearby escape for some entertainment and pampering.

The hotel's 207 comfortable rooms, meeting halls and main ballroom all underwent extensive renovations in the mid-1990s, which have given the hotel its current elegant, inviting look.

Jaketic says the change to Howard Johnson ownership brought additional benefits, including the big hotel chain's reservation system, name recognition and marketing, advertising and quality assurance programs.

He says the hotel takes pride in meeting and exceeding standards.

"We want our guests to be as comfortable as possible, make themselves at home and enjoy their stay in one of Canada's great hotels."

HALTON
Region of Prosperity

With robust employment growth, easy highway access to major centres and a wealth of parks, Halton is truly a region of diversity and prosperity.

In terms of efficient, convenient highway access, Halton is one of Canada's best-connected regions with superb access to Hamilton, Niagara and Toronto.

To the north are the east-west corridors of highways 401, 407 and 5.

To the south lie the east-west highways 403, and Queen Elizabeth Way plus the Plains/York corridor.

Lakeshore boulevards also connect Burlington and Oakville to Toronto and Hamilton shorelines.

Highway 6 and a number of other north-south regional roads connect with Halton's northern communities.

All of Halton's road arteries form an enviable transportation circulation system allowing for swift movement of people, goods and services.

Great highway access and a location on Lake Ontario between Hamilton and Niagara and the Toronto sprawl make Halton an ideal business site.

Halton is within a 400-mile radius of some of the largest population centres and markets in North America.

Businesses are also attracted to Halton's large available land parcels that are priced below tracts in Toronto.

Then there's Halton's impressive quality of life. The region boasts numerous parks and conservation areas and the world-famous Royal Botanical Gardens serves as a gateway of greenery and floral colours linking Burlington and Hamilton.

The region's natural areas include much of the Niagara Escarpment and Camp Nemo, a regional campground, that's home to my own 4th Ancaster Scouts (I serve as Scoutmaster) and to numerous other Scouting groups.

Halton region is comprised of the towns of Milton and Halton Hills (containing Georgetown and Acton), and the cities of Burlington and Oakville. The two cities account for about 80 per cent of employment.

More than 340,000 people make their home in Halton region and the regional population is projected to increased by nearly 45,000 people by 2001, giving it a population of 385,000.

Halton Region 1998 Financial & Economic Survey projections call for a total population of 538,000 by 2016.

In 2016, Burlington's population, now around 138,000 people, is expected to grow to 178,000.

Oakville, with 130,000 people and growing fast, is expected to have a population of 215,000 in 2016, according to projections in the region's 1998 Financial & Economic Survey.

Small businesses account for a growing number of jobs across Canada. This is particularly true in Halton region,

Halton: Region of Prosperity

Enjoying the greenery and waterfront at Burlington's Spencer Smith park.   *- Photo by Paul Sparrow*

which is politically part of the Greater Toronto Area. Much of western Halton region, particularly Burlington, also enjoys strong economic, recreational and cultural ties with Greater Hamilton.

"Two thirds of all employees in the manufacturing and related sectors are employed in companies with 1-10 employees," notes a recent Economic Activity report produced by Business Development Centre offices at the Regional Municipality of Halton.

"As a result, Halton's economic well-being is not dependent on the health of a few large employers," the report concludes.

In the five-year period from 1991 to 1996, Halton's employment increased to 180,895 jobs, a 5.1 per cent increase from 172,095 jobs.

In fact, Halton's employment growth rate from now until 2031 is expected to be higher than the total Greater

Toronto Area growth rate. In 2031, Halton's employment is forecast to be 10 per cent of total GTA employment.

"Employment growth has been most pronounced in Halton Hills with a 12 per cent increase," notes the region's most recent Economic Activity report.

Based on Halton's 1999 Business Directory, the largest industry sectors in the region are Manufacturing and Professional, Scientific and Technical Services which each account for 24 per cent of all companies in Halton.

The Manufacturing sector accounts for 48 per cent of Halton's total workforce of more than 180,000 total employees, while Professional, Scientific and Technical Services account for 11 per cent of the region's total workforce.

The Economic Activity report predicts "Halton's employment growth over the next 35 years will be driven primarily by growth in

activities, which typically locate in business parks, and to a lesser degree by consumer services. Office employment is also expected to rise."

Manufacturing and related activities, which typically occur in industrial areas, are forecasted to "increase dramatically to 245,000 employees in 2031, representing 61 per cent of Halton's total employment."

The report also predicts employment from consumer and government services will "increase substantially as it keeps pace with a surge in population."

"By 2031, consumer and government related services will constitute almost one third of Halton's employment," the report adds.

Halton's office employment is expected to quintuple to 24,000 jobs by the year 3031, accounting for 10 per cent of Halton's total employment growth.

Halton: Region of Prosperity

A glimpse of Burlington's skyline from across the harbour.

- Photo by Paul Sparrow

Enterprise 2000

Halton: Region of Prosperity

A vibrant, colourful paradise stretches before you at the Royal Botanical Gardens.

Enterprise 2000

Halton: Region of Prosperity

- Photo by Paul Sparrow

In the Manufacturing sector, the three largest industries in Halton are Transportation Equipment, fabricated metal products and food. These three industries combined account for over half of all manufacturing employment in Halton region, the report states.

But the Economic Activity report also notes Halton region's economy is diversified more than the economic impact of the big three manufacturing sub-sectors might indicate.

"In spite of the significance of these industries to Halton," the report notes, "Halton is characterized by a very diverse manufacturing base, contributing to Halton's strong, resilient and stable economy."

Halton's employment can also be characterized as stable: There are 43 unions active in Halton region with 269 collective agreements representing 46,671 employees. Yet, in 1997 there were only six work stoppages in Halton involving 2,181 employees.

Numerous employment opportunities can also be found in Halton's growing public sector.

The largest single public sector employer is the Halton Board of Education with 4,700 employees. The separate school board employs 1,720.

Halton's next largest employers: The Regional Municipality of Halton and the Halton regional police force together employ 1,550 people.

Sheridan College employs 1,240 people, Joseph Brant Hospital employs 1,030 and Oakville Trafalgar Hospital employs almost 1,000.

The Economic Activity report concludes that the abundance of public sector jobs is an economic strength.

"The presence of a healthy public sector in Halton means that its economy is somewhat sheltered from economic downturns," the report points out.

Ford Motor Company of Canada has been Halton's largest single employer since the company established in Oakville in 1953. Ford of Canada currently employs more than 5,100

Follow a Royal Botanical Gardens pathway to dreamlike beauty.

- Photo by Paul Sparrow

Halton: Region of Prosperity

people at its Oakville plant.

Other major private sector employers include Maple Leaf Meats, which employs 900 people in Burlington and Karmax Heavy Stamping, which employs 850 people in Milton.

The next largest private sector employers, Cumis Group and Elsag Bailey, each employ around 500.

Employment growth is also evident in the Scientific or high-tech sector where Halton region is home to such advanced technology companies as Gennum Inc., a manufacturer of circuitry and hearing instrument components; Zenon, makers of membrane-based water filtration systems; BCL Magnetics; and CRS Robotics, manufacturers of industrial robots adept at performing the dull, dangerous and dirty jobs – from repetitive tasks to bomb handling – that are deemed unsuited to humans.

Just up the highway in nearby Flamborough is Wescam Inc., makers of camera stabilizing equipment used by the military, rescue operations and, of course, motion pictures.

All of these high-tech leaders are serving niche markets for highly specialized technology. These markets appear to constantly evolve rapidly and mutate into a myriad of newly created opportunities.

Many of these firms employ a few hundred people but have the potential of employing many more as they expand into their markets.

"Only one private sector employer in Halton employs more than 1,000 people," the Economic Activity report observes, "giving further evidence to the fact that Halton's economy is very diversified."

Halton is also a very affluent region.

Of Ontario's regional municipalities, Halton was second only to York in average household income in 1997. Halton averaged $78,287. That's significantly higher than the Ontario average of $60,420.

In average individual income for cities with more than 25,000 taxpayers,

Artist's rendition of the new Reimer office complex.

Oakville placed second highest in all of Canada, behind West Vancouver, with average individual income of more than $41,000 in 1995.

Burlington ranked fifth in Canada with average reported individual income of over $35,000 while the Ontario average was $28,094 and the Canadian average was $25,973.

In keeping with its high household income levels, Halton region also enjoys exceptionally high retail sales per capita that approached $9,000 in the late 1990s.

Building activity has been explosive in Halton region. In 1997, about $670 million worth of building permits were issued, an increase over almost 30 per cent over the previous year's value.

The industrial /commercial sector experienced a strong increase in permit values of 14 per cent and accounted for $172 million.

Halton Hills experienced an astonishing 122 per cent increase in the value of its industrial/commercial permits while Oakville consumed the lion's share of overall value with $94 million in permit value.

As Toronto and Peel regions develop the last of their available lands, it's expected neighbouring Halton region will experience steady increases in its building permits as development pressure moves westward.

One of the biggest single

developments due to open in the new millennium is a new office tower being undertaken by Reimer Construction.

At 250,000 square feet, it will be the largest office complex in Burlington and it represents another milestone in the business history of a prestigious developer who has so transformed the local landscape it's been dubbed Reimer Country.

Business achievement is a common thread in the entire Reimer family. Rudy Reimer's wife Teresa heads a successful interior design company, son Rudy has his own construction firm and son-in-law Randy Heine runs an office tenant services company.

Another intriguing Burlington businessman is Tim Hogan, president of Mercedes-Benz dealership Garden Motorcar, where great service and a relaxed atmosphere go hand in hand. Hogan comes from a family of famous car dealers. The approach he's taking is exactly what Mercedes-Benz needs.

For anyone interested in further researching companies, agencies and organizations cited in this book, I refer you again to the telephone directory at the back of this book.

The directory is provided as a service to researchers and anyone else who may want more information.

Meanwhile, you can read all about the inspiring stories of Hogan, Reimer and the Reimer family, next.

Garden Motorcar

Tim Hogan felt a little uncomfortable visiting some of the luxury car dealerships in Toronto.

"I pulled up to this one dealership in particular," Hogan recalls, "and as I walked to the door I saw all the sales people inside were wearing expensive suits and jewelry."

"To be quite honest, I felt a bit under-dressed, maybe even a little intimidated – so I turned around and I left," he adds, shaking his head at the absurdity of the 1994 moment.

Hogan was no ordinary customer: He was and is part of an industry-savvy family of auto dealers. He wasn't there to buy a car. He was shopping for an entire dealership.

He still has trouble believing that someone with his background could feel out of place in an auto showroom.

"The experience told me that there had to be a better way of selling cars."

Hogan, 60, grew up around cars. In the late 1960s through the early 1980s, he ran a Ford dealership with his father, the late Jack Hogan. In 1983, he began operating a Chev-Olds dealership in Brampton while brother Ainslie Hogan ran Dixie Ford.

But by the early 1990s, Tim Hogan was again ready for a change.

"I really wanted to get involved in a smaller operation so I could personally staff it and provide high levels of service and attention to people who buy a wonderful automobile," he recollects. "Buying a Mercedes-Benz dealership was a great opportunity."

After encountering an uncomfortable sales atmosphere at some Toronto area dealerships, Hogan found what he was looking for in Burlington.

In the fall of 1994, he bought Garden Motorcar, a Mercedes-Benz dealership on Plains Road West, near Hamilton.

"I'm from Toronto but I really like it here," Hogan asserts enthusiastically.

"The Burlington-Hamilton area is very down to earth, unpretentious."

Hogan delights in bringing these qualities into his spacious showroom. Sales people are presentable in dress shirts and slacks. But there's a welcome absence of three-piece imported suits and costly jewelry.

"We don't overdress. It starts with me and you'll find it with our entire staff," says Hogan. "It's a friendly atmosphere. Buying a Mercedes-Benz should be an enjoyable experience."

Hogan notes, "everyone is attended to in a relaxed manner. People who visit us often dress in casual attire. We want them to be comfortable."

> "It starts with me and you'll find it with our entire staff. It's a friendly atmosphere. Buying a Mercedes-Benz should be an enjoyable experience."

The warm sense of laidback comfort is evident in the dealership's whole approach. This is very much a family company with Hogan's wife Debbie handling customer relations. Son Michael is sales manger and daughter Kelly is a sales representative.

While all Mercedes-Benz dealerships sell their cars for the same prices, the dealerships can differ on service.

That's where Hogan likes to excel.

"I love to compete on service, our whole staff does. We take a lot of pride in providing the best service possible and that's a great benefit to clients."

Service includes follow-up calls to customers by Debbie Hogan who checks to see if they're satisfied with the vehicle and service received.

"When the wife of the owner takes a personal role in customer relations, it sends a message to staff that we mean business – we want full customer satisfaction," says Tim Hogan.

Hogan's down-to-earth approach is exactly what Mercedes-Benz needs as it enters the new millennium.

In the early 1990s, Mercedes-Benz lost some market share to lower-priced Japanese luxury cars.

Mercedes-Benz fought back by making model changes every 5-7 years instead of every 10 years. The cars were modernized with numerous added features, including front, rear and side airbags, enhanced traction control – even coffee cup holders.

Despite an array of added-value features, there have been minor price increases for the past five years and some of the most expensive Mercedes-Benz models have actually dropped in price by as much as $15,000.

And the number of models has grown. There is still the entry level Mercedes-Benz C-Class starting at $38,000 plus the mid-range E-Class from $60,000 and the S-Class starting at $90,000. But now there are niche models fitting in between the three basic model lines. In fact, a sport utility vehicle is now a top-seller.

In successfully recovering and expanding its market share, Mercedes-Benz doubled worldwide production of its cars to 1 million from 500,000.

Garden Motorcar now has an inventory with many vehicles on display. When Hogan bought the dealership in 1994, it had annual sales of 60 vehicles from 15,000 square feet of combined showroom, service and office space. It now enjoys annual sales of about 300 vehicles from 22,000-square-foot premises.

"These are also terrific looking cars – this is not your grandfather's Mercedes," Hogan asserts, a hand resting on a new convertible.

"It's a winning formula. We now offer a range of models with a lot of features while still providing a very safe, well-built vehicle that will retain much of its value for years to come."

> ➤ *Tim Hogan wants to put you comfortably behind the wheel of a Mercedes-Benz.*

Garden Motorcar

- *Photo by Paul Sparrow*

Enterprise 2000

Reimer Country

Few people know the inspiring story behind Rudy Reimer, a developer who has so transformed the landscape it's been dubbed 'Reimer Country'.

Reimer is the multi-millionaire developer of many of bold glass office complexes lining the Queen Elizabeth Way from Burlington through to Oakville.

He's also the patriarch of a family of successful business leaders that includes wife Teresa, head of T. Reimer Design Consultants Inc.; son Rudy, president of R. K. Reimer Developments; and son-in-law Randy Heine, president of Crystal Ridge Development Services.

As he surveys the stretching landscape from the glass walls of his penthouse office, Reimer, 62, exudes the self-confidence of a savvy dealmaker and developer who has achieved an enviable degree of business success.

But how he rose to his position of power and influence is one of the most intriguing and inspiring stories you're ever likely to read.

Reimer's life story begins in Ukraine where he was born to a Mennonite German family that spoke a Low German dialect, similar to Dutch. At school, Reimer had to learn Russian to comprehend classroom instruction.

The family lived a crowded existence in a house offering less than 700 square feet of living space – about the size of his current bathroom.

As a religious minority in Ukraine, the Reimer family was subjected to persecution. And it soon intensified.

In the early 1940s, with World War II raging, the Russians periodically walked into his home and removed a family member for questioning. Jail terms often followed. Some were never seen or heard from again.

"Then," Reimer recalls, "when I was about six years old, the Germans came marching in. They told us: 'You're Germans – you're coming with us,' and we were taken to Germany."

Much of their 200-mile journey was on foot across rough terrain.

"I can remember walking past Dresden and through Berlin when these cities were being bombed," he recalls nearly 50 years later in an interview at his penthouse office.

> "Then, when I was about six years old, the Germans came marching in. They told us: 'You're Germans – you're coming with us,' and we were taken to Germany."

"What I remember most is how the cities lit up when they were bombed, and the glow as they burned," he adds.

Although a peaceful Mennonite, his father, Peter Reimer, was forced to join the German army – the alternative to not enlisting was a bullet to head – and he was sent to the Russian front.

The Russians in the dying months of the war captured Peter Reimer. When they questioned him, he answered first in German, then in Russian. This proved to be a nearly fatal mistake.

It led his captors to accuse him of being a spy. A gun was pointed towards his head. The trigger was pulled. A bullet shot through his hat.

Having cheated death, Peter Reimer was allowed to live – serving a life sentence as a Siberian Gulag prisoner.

"We didn't even know he'd been captured," Reimer recalls.

By this point, Reimer was 8 years old. He was left with his mother Anna and sisters Frida, 4, and Mary Anne, 2.

The war ended, but the Reimer family's troubles continued. Anna Reimer was questioned by the Russian occupiers and made her husband's mistake of answering them in Russian. She was taken away for questioning.

She was released temporarily after a prominent relative intervened. She was told to return to the police station the following morning.

"My mother knew where this was likely to end up," Reimer asserts, "so she decided we would all escape from the Russian sector of Berlin."

Anna Reimer and her three children walked in the dark to the train station where the family hid in the bushes.

As the train pulled into the station and slowed down, the mother and her three children crawled quickly between the slowly moving wheels of a boxcar, emerging on the other side where the boxcar doors were located.

"My mother knocked, the door opened and we were pulled inside," Reimer recollects.

"A moment later, the door was wrenched open and a guard pointed a gun at us. He said he didn't remember us getting on the train and demanded a passenger count. One of the men in our boxcar told him there would be no counting as everyone was legally on board. The guard shrugged and left."

Once they were safely in what was then West Germany, Reimer excelled in school, skipped several grades.

Three years later, the family immigrated to Canada and integrated into a small Mennonite community at Vineland, Ontario, in 1949.

They later discovered Peter Reimer was still alive. With help from the Mennonite congregation, Anna Reimer arranged for a meeting with Russian leader Nikita Khrushchev during his 1962 visit to the United States. Khrushchev personally intervened and returned Peter Reimer to his family.

Rudy Reimer was 23 when his father returned after 18 years in prison.

Reimer was also, by this point, forging impressive success in business.

> ➤ Son-in-law Randy Heine, son Rudy and wife Teresa stand behind Rudy Reimer.

Reimer Country

- Photo by Paul Sparrow

Enterprise 2000

Reimer Country

Starting up a construction firm was an easy decision for Rudy Reimer. He liked working on homes.

"In 1954, I worked about a year for a contractor in the Vineland area, doing everything from painting basement walls to laying kitchen tiles," he adds.

"Then a year later, at age 18, I went into business as a subcontractor working for the same contractor. I had 40 people working for me. I was able to do the work at less cost and I doubled the money I was making."

By 1957, Reimer decided it was time to take the next step and he became a general contractor, taking over the business of C. P. Unrau who retired.

Reimer didn't have much start up capital. But he did have someone who believed in this ambitious young man.

Robert Johnson, president of the Penn Cashway in Grimsby, had told Reimer he would help him get started.

"He told me if there was every anything I needed, to contact him," Reimer recalls, "so I went to him and asked him to lend me $250,000."

"Mr. Johnson wrote a cheque for $250,000 and as he handed it to me, he told me it was his retirement money so if I blew it he'd have worked his whole life for nothing. I paid him back in six months with 6 per cent interest."

Reimer went on to build 500 homes across Niagara and Hamilton areas, including the homes of prominent doctors and dentists and the Auch Mar neighbourhood on Hamilton Mountain.

Building largely in the Grimsby area, he constructed starter, move-up and retirement homes for repeat customers.

In 1962, serviced land had become scarce in the Grimsby area. But he had several developments in Burlington, so Reimer made the move to Burlington.

He built a number of executive homes in the Tyandaga area, including his own palatial home. A 1970 open house drew 12,000 people, police crowd control and a lot of publicity.

In fact, Reimer often moves into one of his homes in the neighbourhoods he builds. He's lived in 30 houses since

Rudy Reimer shares a happy moment with U.S. President George Bush.

the age of 20 and he often sells his personal homes fully furnished. His current home features a 3,000-square-foot bedroom, larger than most homes.

In 1972, Reimer had already built more than 2,000 homes when he was encouraged by the City of Burlington to take on commercial development.

He built an office and warehousing building at Mainway and Blair Road.

Next came a commercial building housing the Royal Bank, on Harvester Road, east of Guelph Line.

He became a full-service developer, acquiring raw land, servicing it, developing it, financing and promoting the development and selling the finished product. He also manages and leases some commercial complexes.

"That's the way we continue to do business," Reimer explains. "When you can do the whole thing – you can make more money down the road."

In 1990, Reimer began building the impressive office towers off Burloak Drive where the penthouse headquarters of Reimer Construction

are located. Many of his buildings are sold to investors while he manages the complexes. He now looks after more than $100 million in real estate assets.

He's leased out 100 per cent of the space in a newly completed 100,000-square foot office tower and has drawn major corporations as tenants, each occupying an entire floor.

He's also starting a convention centre in the Burloak Business Park that will seat 900 people. It features three main halls and two boardrooms. Occupancy is to take place in 2000 and there already bookings for conventions.

Reimer attributes his company's enduring success to his staff, his investors, his tenants and the people who have believed in him and supported his career in one way or another over the years. And he believes in adding value to his work.

"I think one of the reasons we have been successful is that we always try to exceed the expectations of our investors, our tenants and everyone else who does business with us."

Reimer Country

He was born the son of wealthy developer. But there were no shortcuts for Rudy K. Reimer. His rise to success literally began at ground level.

"I started out in the construction business pushing a broom," Reimer recalls with a smile. "I was about eight years old and being a little guy, I swept out a lot of the crawl spaces in the homes my dad built."

"Then I graduated to sweeping out whole houses," chuckles the son of developer Rudy Reimer.

"When I got a little older, I was paid $4-a-lawn to cut the grass at my father's housing developments," adds the 41-year-old president of R. K. Reimer Developments in an interview at his penthouse office in a commercial tower his company built.

"Then I realized I could make a lot more money with a lot less work if I subcontracted the work out and paid other kids $2-a-lawn."

That may have been the first entrepreneurial spark from Rudy K. Reimer. But it wouldn't be the last from a developer who has achieved an enviable degree of success on his own.

His firm is completely independent of Reimer Construction and has earned a reputation as a leading developer.

As a youngster growing up in Burlington, Reimer had the advantage of being more focused than most peers.

"I always knew I'd be in the family business and I tended to concentrate more on that than on my schoolwork at times," he recalls. "By Grade 12, I knew more about framing houses than math. But this is a constant learning experience and I later became good at math because I use it a lot in building."

Indeed, Reimer and his company are known for the exacting standards they apply to building construction. Lasers are routinely used to establish precise angles and the buildings themselves are designed to feature a number of angles, affording many terrific views.

Reimer established his company in 1979 and it has gone on to achieve considerable success in the ensuing decades. The company does projects on behalf of Reimer Construction along with its own projects. It also does all of the property maintenance for all 20 Reimer buildings.

"My father will often come up with a concept and design and he'll do a feasibility study," Reimer explains.

Strict attention to details and a desire to add value and exceed expectations are common threads tying the various Reimer Country companies together.

"Then, I'll fine tune the design and make sure it's cost-effective and that the layout is functional. I'll improve the design if necessary and build the best project possible."

Randy Heine grew up in the construction business. So it's not surprising that he met, and married, the daughter of a developer.

"In my family, we were born with a shovel in our hand," laughs Heine, 40, the president of Crystal Ridge Development Services and husband of Rudy Reimer's daughter Darlene.

Heine's company is an independent firm that is associated with Reimer Construction and performs much of the post-construction service work associated with Reimer projects.

At age 20, Heine had worked as a painting subcontractor and by his mid-twenties; he'd painted a number of the Reimer buildings. This experience led to more work and set the footings for starting his own firm to serve tenants.

"We're kept very busy," he notes.

Teresa Reimer has a proven knack for creating powerful yet warm decors that are infused with an understated opulence.

"We include decorative columns, mirrors and woodwork to achieve an interesting and formal yet warm look," explains the president of T. Reimer Design Consultants Inc.

"I like what can best be described as a neo-classical look using pillars and marble – it's a blend of classical and modern influences," adds Reimer, 36, in an interview at her penthouse office in the same tower housing the business interests of husband Rudy Reimer Sr.

Although she occasionally performs contract work outside of Reimer Construction, most of Teresa Reimer's interior design work involves the commercial complexes owned and/or managed by her husband.

"It's more than enough to keep me very busy," Reimer says with a laugh, her subdued accent revealing a trace of her Atlanta, Georgia roots.

"After all," she adds, "we've got more than a million square feet of space to see to in 20 buildings with 110 tenants. And there are often new tenants moving into our buildings."

"I also enjoy listening to our tenants and helping them out by meeting their needs," adds Teresa Reimer, who married Rudy Reimer in 1989 after meeting him on a cruise ship in the early 1980s.

"I like getting the tenants' input so the design of their offices reflects what they want as well as what we want."

Strict attention to details and a desire to add value and exceed expectations are common threads tying the various Reimer Country companies together.

With such laudable shared values in place, these independent companies are well positioned to take on and conquer any challenges the new millennium may bring their way.

Overleaf: A Reimer office tower.

Enterprise 2000

FINANCIAL ADVISORS

Most of us are running on a workweek treadmill chasing the Canadian dream. We live a paycheque-to-paycheque existence.

We barely cope with demands of daily life. We know we're getting on in years. We also know it's important to financially plan our future. But few of us can find time.

And that's precisely why financial planning by professional advisors has become a major growth industry.

As we age, there's a growing acceptance – however reluctant – of our own mortality. And it's coupled with a clear, somber understanding that we need to take steps today to ensure tomorrow doesn't bring a life of poverty.

There's also a growing realization that government pensions and benefits may fall seriously short of meeting our actual needs and expectations.

We know we need to take measures now to independently see to our future needs.

And many of us turn to professional financial planners.

"Financial management services represent an absolutely huge industry," notes Neil Everson, manager of business development for Hamilton-Wentworth region.

"The baby boomers are not only generating great wealth, they're inheriting great wealth as well," adds Everson, citing studies that indicate Canada's baby boom generation will inherit over $2-trillion in passed–on wealth.

David Foot, author of Boom, Bust & Echo, suggests the baby boomers will come to dominate the financial sector.

And Lee Kirkby, former executive director of the Hamilton & District Chamber of Commerce, notes the public's growing interest in financial matters is already making itself felt.

"All you have to do is check out a retirement planning seminar," Kirkby observes, "and you'll find hundreds of people in attendance."

"The enormous growth of the financial planning service sector," Kirkby adds, "is in large part a response to specialization."

"As things become more complicated, there's a realization it's becoming too complex to deal with on our own," he says.

"That's when we turn to financial experts to help build our wealth and our pensions while we concentrate on the things we do best."

One of the most thorough area financial experts is Armando Vacca; a financial planner who takes a holistic approach that encompasses all aspects of life, not just money matters.

Financial planner Jerry Santucci has modeled his approach after one of the world's richest investors, Warren Buffett.

And the financial planners at Bick Financial Security put a strong emphasis on serving the community they grew up in.

We'll learn more about these skilled professionals, next.

A. D. Vacca and Associates

Money isn't everything: The obvious truth in this familiar cliché can be too easily pushed aside in a single-minded struggle to make more money.

For many, money issues become overriding concerns leaving little room for family or friends.

Money isn't everything: It's a cliché that has been taken to heart by Armando David Vacca, a financial planner who believes charting your financial future is only part of his job.

Couples turning up for Vacca's financial advice have sometimes revealed problems that run deeper than paying today's bills and saving for tomorrow's retirement. Money concerns can distract from severe communication problems. They can mask a marriage in trouble.

"Money can certainly be a divisive issue that can undermine families if left unaddressed," Vacca notes in an interview at his Hamilton office.

"But it can also be a distraction, taking your attention away from largely non-financial problems that can also undermine families," he adds.

"We try to bring an element of marriage counseling into the financial planning process," explains the president of A. D. Vacca & Associates, Financial Planning Group.

"We've had marriages strengthened and saved here, real breakthroughs in communication, and I'm thankful to have played a role but the power comes from a higher source," adds Vacca, a devout follower of Christian values of kindness, compassion and fair play.

In many ways, Vacca can more aptly be described as a life planner, a role borne of years of incorporating all aspects of personal well being into the financial planning process.

When explaining this process to clients, Vacca sketches a triangle of life, with each equal side representing an area of well-being: Health/spiritual, wealth/work and family/social.

If any of the three, interconnected areas isn't well, its illness can spread to the remaining two. A family/social problem, such as a troubled marriage, can impact on health-spiritual health and be a distraction in building the wealth-work side. Too narrow a focus on wealth/work is often at the expense of family/social and health/spiritual.

> Due to the interconnected nature of the triangle of life and the relationships of couples, Vacca prefers not to deal with one family member in isolation when mapping out plans for financial health.

"I always try to work with couples, together, to get a good sense of their total needs," he explains.

This effort to gain insight into all aspects of the couple's triangle of life often results in more than a thorough financial plan or saved marriage.

"We like to go beyond offering investment advice - we're very pleased that we've been able to help people make a successful career transition as well," says Vacca who notes 18-20 per cent of his clientele is self-employed.

Vacca, a past president of the Hamilton-Niagara chapter of CAFP (Canadian Association of Financial Planners), manages over $50 million in assets on behalf of his clients, ably assisted by a staff of five at his expanded Queenston Road offices.

Of the over 1,900 mutual funds on the market, Vacca selects just 150 funds within the top 12 fund families. His general approach is to build wealth gradually with modest risk. But each Client's financial plan is custom-made.

Vacca's sensitivity to the complex financial needs of families was learned the hard way at an early age: He was still in his late teens when his father died suddenly of a heart attack.

The 1976 death of Pasqualino Vacca left his family in emotional and financial chaos. The responsibility of dealing with family finances fell on the shoulders of the eldest son. It was a turning point in Armando Vacca's life.

At age 19, when most of his peers were enjoying carefree lives, Vacca found himself growing up fast, sorting out the complexities of his family's finances and future needs. He recalls it as an intensive learning period that profoundly changed his life.

"I was motivated to bring about some security for my family," Vacca recalls. "I didn't want to see other families go through this chaos. Out of that tragedy came a sense of purpose."

"My family was unprepared for the future and I found others similarly unprepared. The realization these problems existed catapulted me into financial planning. I had found my mission in life."

He completed in a three-year Business Administration program at Mohawk College in 1980. He became licensed to sell life and disability insurance and mutual funds and went into financial planning, starting Money Concepts (Stoney Creek) in 1988.

Vacca, CFP, R.F.P. (Certified Financial Planner and Registered Financial Planner), has never forgotten the crisis his own family encountered. While other planners only deal with wealthy clients, he extends his services to middle-income Canadians.

"We're offering financial planning for the unchauffered and yachtless," smiles Vacca who has broadened his client base to help families of ordinary means achieve financial independence.

The approach has given Vacca a growing business, based heavily on referrals from satisfied clients.

➤ *Armando Vacca learned from his family's financial crisis and now helps other families.*

A. D. Vacca and Associates

- *Photo by Paul Sparrow*

Enterprise 2000

Jerry Santucci & The Berkshire Group

"Only a small percentage of the population retires rich - but there are steps you can take to beat those odds," asserts financial planner Jerry Santucci.

"To do well financially - corporately or personally - the investment plan and philosophy must be solid, clearly mapped out, and followed closely," he adds.

Santucci, financial advisor and wealth management specialist with Berkshire Securities Inc., takes a measured, go-slow approach towards creating financial independence.

"There's nothing wrong with getting rich slowly," Santucci smiles during an interview at his North Service Road, Burlington office.

"A financial plan is gradual process - not a single event," adds Santucci who had amassed about $55-million in clients' investments under his administration by the year 2000. By the late 1990s, his clientele had doubled to 500 groups and individuals.

Santucci, 42, draws inspiration from billionaire investor Warren Buffett.

Buffett's 1993 net worth of $8-billion US nearly tripled by 1997 to $23.2-billion US as estimated in the July 28, 1997 issue of Forbes magazine. In its October 1998 issue, Forbes estimated Buffett's wealth at over $29-billion US. Even conservative estimates place his net worth at $40 billion US by 2000. By the late 1990s, buying one share in Buffett's Berkshire Hathaway holding firm cost $78,000 US, up from $30,000 US in 1996.

"Buffett is the richest investor of all time, he's our role model and we study his recipe for success," notes Santucci. Berkshire derives its name and inspiration from Buffett's Berkshire Hathaway company, although there is no affiliation of any kind.

What are the ingredients to the Buffett recipe?

"Well," Santucci answers, "first you should acquire an ownership stake in outstanding, well-managed companies in growth industries."

"Then, hold onto it for a very long time," adds Santucci. "Buffett's own favorite investment time span is forever. That way, you defer taxes on your investment and it keeps growing."

Further criteria, he adds, includes never buying into a firm with products or services you don't understand.

"You should also avoid cyclical or resource-based companies and stick with proven earners with strong balance sheets and a history of consistent, predictable earnings and cash flow."

In 1994, Santucci recruited Donna Waggoner and Paul Masotti, who have worked alongside Santucci whose vision was to build a wealth management team second to none.

Waggoner, who is the client services manager, also handles marketing and public relations. Masotti has worked very successfully as Santucci's sales associate. The team also includes Odete Pascoa; administration, and Josephine Zeller, sales associate.

In 1998, to better serve his client's growing needs, Donald Bell, then associate vice-president of The Berkshire Group, joined Santucci's team. Bell brought a wealth of knowledge and expertise to the team.

Bell, a lawyer, had served as a legal and technical information resource for The Berkshire Group head office personnel. He was responsible for head office compliance matters. He trained personnel and served as an expert in taxation and financial planning.

One of Bell's great strengths is in the area of estate planning, including the establishment of wills and trusts. These invaluable services are all the more timely as the baby boom generation ages. Bell's estate planning

expertise particularly shines in regard to more complex personal and business situations. He's also an expert in taxation, life insurance and pensions.

The team is capable of delivering expert assistance in virtually any finance-related, life-planning area.

Santucci and his team also know the value of educating their clients to make them active participants in their own financial future.

"We explain our philosophy, based on Buffett's established investment practices," says Santucci, "and then we develop a plan to meet their needs. Our objective is to maximize their returns while minimizing their risks."

Santucci recommends money managers who closely follow Buffett's long-term investment approach. An example would be AIC Mutual Funds.

Chairman Michael Lee-Chin - who has been an inspiration to Santucci - has turned AIC into a powerful mutual fund company. While affiliated with AIC, Berkshire is an independent dealer with over 60 offices across Canada and a network of 250 sales representatives.

"We use Buffett as the model and by applying his criteria, we eliminate most of the investments out there, to concentrate on the investing in the best companies around," explains Santucci who shops the market for managers who adhere to Buffett principles and for mutual funds that are worthy of being purchased and held many years.

As one of Berkshire's top-performing Gold Circle Club members, Santucci became intrigued at an early age with the dynamics of successful investing.

Santucci, who grew up in Hamilton and now resides in Burlington, earned a BA in economics from Western University at London, Ontario.

In 1983, he joined the Investors Group and became a successful financial advisor and seller of mutual funds. The funds can contain stocks, bonds, Guaranteed Investment Certificates and other investments.

Jerry Santucci & The Berkshire Group

Team Santucci arrives with confidence to solve any financial planning problem.   *Photo by Michael Dismatsek*

He left Investors in 1992 to join Berkshire where he's licensed to sell mutual funds, insurance, securities and tax shelters. Santucci soon furthered his reputation as a conscientious financial advisor who builds investment portfolios based on each client's needs.

Santucci employs a thorough approach that includes collecting the client's financial and personal data, determining goals and commitments,

explaining investment philosophy and making investment recommendations.

He acts as a guide, navigating the client through a mutual funds industry that has grown from $4 billion in the early 1980s to $325-billion in 1999.

"There's a proliferation of products out there - I try to cut through the confusion and create an investment strategy that's right for the client," he explains.

Santucci also advises keeping your

cool when stock prices suddenly dip.

"I don't think volatility is risk - not if the stock meets Buffett's criteria."

Santucci is clearly committed to following what he sees as a winning investment formula. And he's committed to more than meeting financial planning industry standards.

"We want to go far beyond the minimum standards imposed by the regulators - we want to blow away the standards by exceeding expectations."

Bick Financial Security

Many people devote little time to one of life's most important issues: Their own financial security.

Surveys suggest most Canadians will spend more time watching TV in an evening than they'll spend on financial planning in a whole year.

Although few would argue against the importance of building financial security, life's more trivial matters easily distract us.

Financial planning seems to be a matter we'd rather not consider.

Fortunately, the subject of building a secure financial future garners a lot of thoughtful consideration at Bick Financial Security Corporation.

"We spend a lot of time on long-term portfolio planning and keeping current with investment products," notes Leonard Bick, a managing partner with the Ancaster-based firm.

"Our mission is to help clients achieve financial security," he adds in an interview at the company's office in a stone building on Wilson Street.

Bick, 43, notes most people are happy to let a professional plan out their financial future while they get on with their day-to-day lives.

Even those rare individuals who take a strong interest and prefer to do their own financial planning can find the task daunting, observes Bick, who, along with older brother Clarence, 44, is a principal in the firm.

"Our clients are becoming more sophisticated and knowledgeable, but the rate of change goes beyond the ability of most people to keep pace," Bick notes. "Even for those of us in the business, staying current with all of the changes can be a challenge, but we work very hard at keeping up."

Joining the Bicks is a team of financial planners, including Bernice Cairns, a certified management accountant; George Van Arragon; Brian Johnson; and Dr. John Knechtel. Financial planner Melissa DeBrouwer heads the firm's Milton branch office.

All of these financial planners take a conservative approach to building wealth on behalf of clients. Investment strategies tend to be long-term. But each client's financial plan is tailored to meet his or her specific needs.

The Bick brothers, Cairns, Johnson, Van Arragon and Knechtel take a three-step planning approach.

> "We spend a lot of time on long-term portfolio planning and keeping current with investment products… Our mission is to help clients achieve financial security."

The first step involves sitting down with the client for an informal interview to clarify and quantify the client's goals and objectives.

Next, a strategy is developed to help the client reach goals and objectives.

Finally, the Bick financial advisor will recommend specific financial products to help implement your financial strategy. The planner will also monitor the progress of the client's financial portfolio and provide ongoing advice via periodic reviews.

One of Bick Financial's strengths is that it's an independent company that is not tied to a particular mutual fund.

This means the Bick brothers; Cairns, Johnson, Van Arragon and Knechtel are free to search out the best products from more than 1,000 of the top mutual funds on the market.

They can also choose the most promising GICs (Guaranteed Investment Certificates) from 30 trust companies and select from a variety of other investment devices such as segregated funds, bonds and labour sponsored investment funds, providing the ability to achieve a product mix most suited to the client's needs. Assisting the financial planners and their clients is a support staff of 21.

Another great strength at Bick Financial is the company's community ties. Both Bick brothers, Knechtel, Cairns and Johnson reside in Ancaster. Van Arragon lives in Hamilton's neighboring West Mountain. They sponsor several local youth sports teams and they're members of several service clubs, including Rotary and the Ancaster division of the Hamilton and District Chamber of Commerce.

Their Wilson Street building is also a local landmark and is a recognized part of Ancaster's architectural heritage. Known historically as the Carriage Works, the building had been used since the 1860s to build horse-drawn carriages. In 1885, the existing stone structure was built on the foundations of the original building after it was destroyed in a fire.

Leonard and Clarence Bick grew up in Ancaster and later attended nearby McMaster University where they each earned MBAs in the early 1980s. They also hold CFP (Certified Financial Planner) and RFP (Registered Financial Planner) certifications.

In 1987, the Bick brothers already had several years financial planning experience when they became managers of the Hamilton offices of Financial Concept Group.

Then, in 1993, they took over the Ancaster FCG offices and founded the Bick Financial Security firm.

The firm now manages $180 million in assets on behalf of 2,400 clients.

Leonard Bick says the company may well expand its branch offices but remains committed to Ancaster.

"This is our home town and it's where we want to be. Instead of spending hours commuting – we'd rather spend that time on our clients."

> ➤ *Clarence and Leonard Bick with Brian Johnson, Bernice Cairns, John Knechtel and George Van Arragon at Bick Financial in Ancaster.*

Bick Financial Security

- *Photo by Paul Sparrow*

Enterprise 2000

Hamilton, at the head of Lake Ontario, is a prosperous centre of opportunity.

- Photo by Paul Sparrow

THE ENTREPRENEURS

With small businesses accounting for most jobs in the new millennium, the role of innovative entrepreneurs has become vitally important.

Today's entrepreneurs are tomorrow's employers. Acting on an idea, they create their own job. With success, other jobs follow.

"The trend is for home-based businesses to continue to grow and small businesses to maintain their role as the leading source of jobs in our economy," notes John Dolbec, executive director of the Hamilton & District Chamber of Commerce.

Dolbec suggests the central role of small businesses, as creators of jobs and wealth will increase, thanks in large part to technology.

"Computers have made possible a huge number of home-based businesses," Dolbec observes, "and where you once needed an office with support staff to accomplish certain tasks, now an individual working from home on a computer can accomplish a great deal."

Dolbec says the ability of a home computer to quickly transmit information, faxes and documents marks a quantum leap in the business capabilities of home-based companies.

Instantaneous Internet and e-mail transmissions of large amounts of information have slashed the costs of communication in the information age.

The efficiencies are staggering – and they're about to become even more pronounced.

"The speed of computers once doubled every 18 months," Dolbec recalls. "Now it's doubling every nine months – and soon it will double every three months."

Increased operating efficiencies aren't the only factors driving the rise in entrepreneurialism.

Increased demand for business relationships is a made-to-measure phenomenon favouring entrepreneurs.

"Today's customers are sophisticated," Dolbec observes in an interview at the Hamilton & District Chamber of Commerce offices overlooking Hamilton's recreational waterfront. "Most customers are knowledgeable. They know what they want and they place a premium on value and relationships."

Establishing, enhancing and maintaining personal relationships with clients is often easier for an individual than faceless corporations.

"Relationship management skills with employees and with customers are more and more in demand," Dolbec notes, "and employees are going from being considered an expendable resource to an investment providing valuable skills sets."

Small businesses, including many home-based businesses, have become a huge, growing source of chamber membership.

The Entrepreneurs

Start-up businesses get needed help at GHTEC and the Business Advisory Centre.   *- Photo by Paul Sparrow*

As a result, the chamber is taking on many small business issues, increasing the influence of small firms in the process.

"We're one of the oldest chambers of commerce in Canada and we're now a small business organization," Dolbec points out. The Hamilton chamber has 1,100 company members and 1,600 individual members who together employ more than 50,000 people.

"Small business is where our employment growth has been coming fro and it's an incubator for future growth in jobs and business," he adds.

"After all, 82 per cent or more of the firms in greater Hamilton have ten employees or less," Dolbec notes.

"Stelco and Dofasco now employ half the people they did in the 1970s. The loss of so many jobs would once have been devastated. But our economy is so diverse now; other job opportunities in other sectors have lessened the impact. A lot of these alternative jobs can be attributed to the growing numbers of Hamilton area small businesses and entrepreneurs.

Neighbouring Halton region is also experiencing explosive growth in the sheer numbers of start-up small businesses and entrepreneurs.

Many of these firms employ a few hundred people but have the potential of employing many more as they expand into their markets.

"Only one private sector employer in Halton employs more than 1,000 people," Halton region's Economic Activity report observes, "giving further evidence to the fact that Halton's economy is very diversified."

There's no question entrepreneurs are driving the economy, creating many new jobs in the process.

But why are entrepreneurs suddenly plentiful? Where are they coming from and how are they being created?

Dolbec observes that with the downsizing of many workforces in the 1980s through 1990s, numerous workers were displaced by corporations in an effort to lower company-operating costs and improve cost-efficiency.

"Globalization and accelerated technological change have also had a disruptive impact on some jobs," Dolbec notes.

Merger mania also played a role in wiping out employment. In an attempt to become more competitive, one company would swallow another whole, then spit out half the combined workforce to generate cost savings, which then went towards the cost of financing the merger. Studies have shown that 90 per cent of mergers fail to achieve their set objectives and

The Entrepreneurs

Mohawk College takes pride in its close ties to the business community

succeed only in destroying many jobs.

The reduced workforce trend became more pronounced during periods of recession and, at times, even during bouts of expansion, as companies shed people in hopes of emerging leaner and more efficient. Automation and a desire to please shareholders with fatter bottom lines also added to the pressure to cut jobs and slice costs.

Uprooted from once stable jobs and unable to find replacement work, many of these workers turned their plight into an advantage: They acted on long-held dreams of running their own business and created their own jobs.

The failure rate of start-up businesses is high. More than half don't survive their first year of business operation.

Most of these overnight business people fail. But enough succeed that their sheer numbers work to expand employment and fuel the economy.

Successful entrepreneurs begin with an idea, expand it into a vision and work hard at making their dream a reality. As Thomas Edison once observed, genius is one per cent inspiration, 99 per cent perspiration.

Dolbec says successful entrepreneurs often have an ability to recognize and anticipate changes in the marketplace.

"Having a strong sense of where market demand is going and keeping on top of trends can be crucial for success. You can't be too preoccupied with producing – you have to also be conscious of the trends around you."

Dolbec notes another factor driving the success of an entrepreneur is the ability to successfully position the company in the marketplace.

"Sometimes this can involve more narrowly defining the niche market you're targeting," he says. "It also means doing everything you can to

differentiate yourself from rivals."

Dolbec says some of the most successful entrepreneurs are able to assert their strengths and assume a leadership role in a niche market.

"You want to set yourself apart from the pack and establish yourself as the best company to deal with when it comes to acquiring the particular products or services you provide."

But the most important qualities needed for entrepreneurial success include a firm belief in yourself and the willingness to work hard to achieve success, Dolbec notes.

"Beyond vision and drive, a good entrepreneur knows how to work on his business rather than in his business," he adds.

"You can't just be the best at producing widgets, you also have to excel at managing your business and provide something of unique value."

The Entrepreneurs

Dolbec also advises an entrepreneur's success over the long term may depend on an ability to handle growth.

"You should be able to run your business well enough to allow you to hire someone to do the labour while you concentrate on running the business. Being willing and able to delegate can be critical to success."

Dolbec notes, "a lot of entrepreneurs have trouble developing a customer oriented mindset. They have to realize it's not enough to provide a great product or service; they also have to concentrate on satisfying the needs of their customers. This sensitivity is probably as important as the creativity, imagination and vision they bring to their business."

Lee Kirkby, Dolbec's predecessor, says many of the most successful entrepreneurs share a creative spark, an all-consuming passion for their chosen business endeavours, fierce dogged perseverance and determination.

"Successful business people I've talked to often refer to a business idea and a business focus which together become an all-consuming passion, driving them to achieve success," notes Kirkby, who served eight years as executive director the Hamilton chamber before accepting a position in 1997 as a vice-president of Leppert Business Systems Inc.

"Great entrepreneurs are able to place a commanding focus on what they're trying to do," he adds, "and they're able to identify opportunities and respond to them in a timely manner. Having talent alone isn't enough. It has to be combined with perseverance and a willingness to act fast to take advantage of market opportunities."

Kirkby also notes "often with limited assets, the successful entrepreneur can take an idea and springboard it into something wonderful."

"And they achieve success financially and in other ways by meeting and exceeding expectations."

Unfortunately, even the brightest ideas and greatest efforts can end in failure, as the collapse of so many start-up businesses attests.

Often, all that is needed for these fledgling enterprises to succeed is a little more time to generate sufficient cash flow.

There can also be a need for some expert advice to resolve business problems before they become life-threatening nightmares for a young, start-up company.

To help fledgling entrepreneurs survive and thrive though those early make-it-or-break-it years, Hamilton-Wentworth built, and continues to sponsor, GHTEC.

The Greater Hamilton Technology Enterprise Centre (GHTEC) acts as an incubator for high-tech oriented start-up firms, particularly in such sectors as automotive parts, advanced materials management, telecommunications, medical devices, food processing and environmental services.

New tenant companies setting up Operations at GHTEC (pronounced Gee-Tek) effectively manage and reduce their costs by sharing secretaries, receptionists, telephone answering services, typing services, photo copiers, fax machines, computer equipment, library resource centre, meeting rooms and other amenities with fellow entrepreneurial tenants at this facility managed by the BAC (Business Advisory Centre).

But the biggest benefit to GHTEC tenants is access via the BAC to experts' know-how through mentoring programs and consulting services.

For nominal fees, these programs bring new business people in contact with over 200 experienced specialists from all areas of business.

These business experts, on loan from 30 large Hamilton firms, provide invaluable, timely technical and business-oriented advice, coaching and consultation to help new firms meet operating challenges and master the process of running a small business.

The $4-million, 40,000-square-foot GHTEC facility has already given a healthy head start to several thousand clients, include Patrick Whyte and Alistair Davie (no relation to the author), the founders of Comtek Advanced Structures, which began as a two-man company and now employs 36 people in the field of repairing composite aircraft components.

Operating and driving GHTEC's services and programs is the BAC itself, a non-profit organization, founding in 1977 by senior members of Dofasco, Stelco and other companies that recognized a need to assist small to mid-sized enterprises in resolving technical or management program challenges.

Big companies got the ball rolling because they recognize the need to produce a skilled workforce. And they recognize the growing role of small business entrepreneurs in creating jobs.

While one company hiring 1,000 people will capture the headlines, thousands of small firms, each hiring one to three people, can actually have a greater, more sustainable impact on employment with the added benefit of further diversifying the local economy.

Studies anticipate that in the year 2000, about 40 per cent of all workers in Canada will be self-employed working at their own companies. And most of these companies will employ fewer than five people.

While the cumulative economic impact of start-up firms is huge, many young companies are fragile entities when they begin life.

Indeed, most of these new firms can't afford to learn from their mistakes because just a few mistakes may be enough to put them right out of business. The BAC provides crucial advice helping new firms get over business hurdles.

Mohawk College and the Michael G. DeGroote School of Business at McMaster University work closely with the business community to

The Entrepreneurs

develop programs that closely meet the hiring needs of many companies.

Both educational institutions keep in constant touch with the business community to stay on top of the shifting needs of corporations.

These close liaison efforts have resulted in programs tailor made to business needs. This interactive relationship is explored in more detail in the New Generation chapter.

To get a personal sense of how many small businesses have sprung up in recent years, you need only look around your own community.

In fact, in my own family, I'm far from alone in starting a small business.

My sister Laura Wysocki runs Country Chocolates, a Cambridge-based confectionary firm creating chocolate flowers, spoons and other gift items for firms and individuals.

My brother Kirby runs his own construction/carpentry-contracting firm in Lethbridge, Alberta.

My brother Randy runs his own tile-setting business at Powell River, B.C.

My brother Cameron runs Joynt Ventures, an Internet merchandise catalogue venture (www.quixtar.com) from his Brandon, Manitoba home.

And my brother-in-law, Paul Cleave, founded and continues to run the rapidly growing Mr. Mugs chain of coffee and baked goods stores. His franchising firm is now a big business and was featured in a profile write-up in my last book, Success Stories.

Micro Aide, the computer consulting company mentioned in my last book Success Stories, has moved from Ancaster to Brantford but continues to provide much of southern Ontario with expert advice, purchasing, program set-up and installation services.

The directory at the back of this book contains telephone numbers of many of these and other firms cited in this book for anyone desiring additional information about these companies.

Other examples of rising small firms include IRD1 (Independent Research and Development One) a software

Michael G. DeGroote at a Bermuda park. — Photo by Philippa Davie

games development firm, and Dining Lifestyles, John Chirico's etiquette consulting and wine appreciation company. Principals at both firms also work at Vineland Estates where they apparently caught the entrepreneurial bug from winery owner John Howard.

Although Howard is profiled in the Niagara chapter, he certainly embodies the spirit of a great entrepreneur.

Developer Rudy Reimer, profiled in the Halton chapter also has a warm and inspiring rags-to-riches story.

In fact, virtually all of the people profiled in this book epitomize the enterprising spirit and every one of them would be a worthy candidate for this Entrepreneurs chapter. But in the interests of producing a book with more than one chapter, I've limited the accompanying entrepreneur profiles to

just three people. But what a trio!

We begin with an inspiring profile story on Michael G. DeGroote, updated from by last visit to Bermuda for Success Stories.

The focus now is on DeGroote's new office backroom services empire.

Then we'll feature Michael H. DeGroote, son of the billionaire businessman, who has achieved his own success as a prominent Burlington developer.

And we'll conclude with a profile story on Ron Joyce, expanded from his Success Stories profile to include a more detailed biography of the remarkable co-founder of the Tim Hortons restaurants empire, founder of Jetport and an Atlantic Canada resort.

For all of these informative and inspiring stories, please turn the page.

Michael G. DeGroote

Michael G. DeGroote, one of the world's biggest businessmen, is building a new empire - aimed at helping small businesses.

From his home in sunny Bermuda, DeGroote, now in his mid sixties, is again shaking the business world's tired palm trees: He's now a major provider of services to small firms that had been virtually ignored.

And in helping these small to mid-sized firms employing five to 500 people, DeGroote is quite happily tapping into an under-developed market for outsourcing administrative service that's worth $250 billion US.

His Century Business Services Inc. firm provides one-stop shopping for over 110,000 smaller firms, taking care of their payroll, hiring, firing, benefits, medical insurance, accounting and other paperwork matters, freeing firms to focus on their business.

Through a series of acquisitions, Century now owns numerous accounting, insurance and benefits firms. The company is now the seventh largest accounting firm in the United States. It provides services through a network following a hub and spokes concept, employing benefits of scale.

Century now has 200 offices in 35 American states. Its accounting unit; Century Small Business Solutions has 650 franchised offices in 47 states.

For many years, all of these services have been available to big firms via giant providers that ignore smaller firms. DeGroote is now providing the same services to the smaller firms, mining a virtually untapped market. "The little guys were paying through the nose for these services, if they could get them at all," DeGroote says in an interview at his Bermuda office.

"As big providers keep raising the bar for the size of firms they'll serve, a lot more firms are left out," he adds.

"We're happy to live off these leftovers. By taking over back office paperwork, we're helping these smaller firms become competitive and grow."

DeGroote shares the details of his latest venture as my wife Philippa and I join him on a stroll through a park near his Westbury (Bermuda) offices.

While my wife takes photos, DeGroote relaxes amid the park's tropical splendour and recounts how he's creating a new business empire.

> "As big providers keep raising the bar for the size of firms they'll serve, a lot more firms are left out. We're happy to live off these leftovers. By taking over back office paperwork, we're helping these smaller firms become competitive and grow."

"As you know, I'm a bit of a deal junkie," DeGroote smiles, recalling that it began when he bought control of the Texas-based Republic Waste Management firm, three months after moving to Bermuda on selling his shares in Laidlaw Inc., the firm he built into a multi-billion-dollar giant.

"I had control - but I had inherited a real dog's breakfast of a company," DeGroote recalls. "It took three years to rebuild it into a viable company."

DeGroote enlisted former competitor Wayne Huizenga, previously chairman of the giant Waste Management Corp.

Huizenga invested in Republic Industries. DeGroote, who had been hands-on managing the company until then, decided to turn operating management of Republic Industries over to Huizenga in May 1995.

At that time, Republic Industries' market capitalization (number of shares issued multiplied by the price per share) rang in at $110 million US.

Two years later market capitalization exceeded $10 billion US. These gains pleased shareholders, particularly the largest single shareholder, DeGroote,

who initially held 49% of the shares.

But DeGroote was still saddled with Republic Environmental, spun out as a separate firm.

A solution arrived in the form of the Alliance Group of insurers.

The privately held Alliance Group wanted to go public and a merger with publicly listed Republic Environmental was seen as the fastest way to a stock market listing. Alliance began pressing DeGroote to make a merger happen.

For DeGroote, the pressure was wonderful. Republic Environmental was barely worth $12 million US. But Alliance was enjoying annual revenue of $35.7 million US - and *they* wanted a merger. DeGroote said yes.

To kick-start the publicly listed International Alliance firm, DeGroote and Huizenga each invested another $5 million US "and we thought the share price might climb from $2 to $6," recalls DeGroote.

Headlines reporting that DeGroote *and* Huizenga were investing millions in the new firm sent share prices soaring to the $40US mark in a few weeks, with demand for the stock exceeding the number of shares issued. A stock split ensued and the shares were selling in 1998 for $18 US each, $36 US on a pre-split basis.

DeGroote renamed Alliance as Century Business Services (CBIZ for short). He remains the largest shareholder with 18% of shares.

"We'll let the small firms concentrate on being entrepreneurs - while we take over their paperwork," asserts DeGroote, "and there's a huge market for these services."

"We have to remove the obstacles, the distractions, and give entrepreneurs the tools they need to succeed. It's vital to free them so they can focus their energy on chasing their dream."

> ➤ *Michael G. DeGroote is building a new business empire in sunny Bermuda.*

Michael G. DeGroote

- *Photo by Philippa Davie*

Enterprise 2000

Michael G. DeGroote

Michael G. DeGroote's success is indeed the stuff legends are made of.

Canadian Business magazine ranked the 100 richest Canadians, listing DeGroote at 15th of 23 billionaires with $1.4 billion, behind newspapers owner Kenneth Thomson. Most of those 23 n billionaires inherited wealth. DeGroote got his the hard way: He earned it.

The same issue of Canadian Business also honoured DeGroote's humble business beginnings. The magazine listed the billionaires in the category of worst first job. DeGroote got first prize for hauling manure.

And DeGroote's ability to amass a vast fortune by his own hands is all the more impressive given the obstacles he faced in his youth.

Born in 1933 on a Belgium farm, Michael George DeGroote saw his childhood stripped of innocence by the brutality of World War II.

He was just 14 years old when his family left war-torn Belgium for Canada in 1948, settling on a tobacco farm in Langton, Ontario, about 60 miles south-west of Hamilton.

"Belgium was in major disarray, caused by the Second World War," he recalls, his gravel voice revealing the barest trace of a Flemish accent.

Faced with a language barrier and a difficult period of adjustment, he took advantage of a now defunct Ontario law allowing youth as young as 14 to drop out of school. He has never attended an Ontario school.

"I think it meant that I had to work twice as hard to succeed.... there really is no substitute for a good education," explains the founder of the Michael G. DeGroote School of Business. He donated $3 million to establish the entrepreneurially-spirited school at McMaster University.

DeGroote's own entrepreneurial spirit emerged just a few years after he arrived in Canada. In the early 1950s, an 18-year-old DeGroote bought his first truck, a two-ton army vehicle, and went into business hauling manure.

By the mid-1950s, DeGroote had expanded his first business to include a second truck and a tractor to work area farms plus four gravel dump trucks to work a Woodstock quarry.

By 1957, he had expanded his fleet to about 30 trucks and formed Langton Contracting Co. Ltd., setting up operations at Elliot Lake, then a booming uranium-mining town.

Two years later, DeGroote made a now legendary acquisition when he borrowed $75,000 to buy Laidlaw Transport Ltd., a small Hagersville trucking firm from Robert Laidlaw.

But DeGroote's emerging business empire was dealt a staggering body blow when a plunge in the uranium market prompted an exodus of people and business from Elliot Lake.

DeGroote tried to rebuild the business. but the financial wounds were too deep. In 1962, Langton Contracting went bankrupt, owing $500,000 to 175 creditors. A year later he declared personal bankruptcy with liabilities exceeding $450,000.

"I kept Laidlaw, but I went from driving Cadillacs and living in a rather nice house to driving a rusty, used car and living in a small rented place," he recalls. "It taught me a lesson that's stayed with me - you can't overextend yourself financially," adds DeGroote.

Months later, he was discharged from bankruptcy, allowing him to get back in business with a clean slate - and no obligation to repay creditors.

But DeGroote's own moral code went beyond legal limits. Within six years, he'd paid back his creditors.

"I know that legally I didn't have to pay people back but I did because I felt it was the right thing to do," he asserts. "These people lent me money in good faith and I felt responsible regardless of what the bankruptcy laws said."

It was the right thing to do - and it proved he was a man of his word.

Laidlaw, purchased with borrowed money, was no overnight success story.

"It was so heavily leveraged that it was six years before I could draw a salary - and it wasn't until I took it

Michael DeGroote amid Bermuda splendour.

public in 1969 that I could get any money out," recalls the former Dundas resident who took 30 years from a 1959 purchase of Laidlaw to make it a $2 billion-a-year giant.

Canada's Grand Acquisitor had purchased some 500 companies on Laidlaw's behalf, transforming Laidlaw in the process. The company, which moved its headquarters to Hamilton and later Burlington, grew to become the third-largest waste management firm in North America, second-largest hazardous waste firm and largest operator of school buses.

Michael G. DeGroote

- Photo by Philippa Davie

For 17 years until 1988, Laidlaw's stock performance was listed as the number one growth stock in Canada.

In 1988, he sold his Laidlaw shares to Canadian Pacific for $500 million.

DeGroote stayed on as the chief executive officer for two more years.

And Laidlaw continued to grow by leaps and bounds to achieve market capitalization of over $6 billion (fifth-largest in Canada) by the time DeGroote resigned in mid-1990.

DeGroote took a huge tax hit - but it was also his last tax hit. He gathered his fortune together and moved to a new home amid the palm trees and gentle breezes of Bermuda. A proud Canadian, he retains his Canadian citizenship and passport. He has been named an Officer of Canada for his sizeable contribution to the country. He also has an Honorary 'Doctor of Law' degree from McMaster University.

The Canadian connections of Michael G. DeGroote, O. C., L.L.D, include $5 million funding for the Michael G. DeGroote Foundation for epilepsy research at McMaster.

His ties also include funding for recreation facilities at McMaster and Hillfield-Strathallan College and, of course, the Michael G. DeGroote School of Business at McMaster where he recently funded a student centre.

DeGroote also spends over two months every year in Canada, mainly in Burlington visiting family, including daughter Joni, son Tim, son Michael Jr. who runs housing development company Westbury International and son Gary who runs GWD Investments.

"I'll never give up my citizenship," DeGroote asserts. "I'm a proud Canadian and Canada is where I earned all my early success."

Michael H. DeGroote

Michael H. DeGroote does more than construct a building: He creates it.

Starting with raw land and a concept, he stays with a project every step of the way, taking it through design and construction phases, right to final sale or lease.

"I like to see a structure being built from scratch to completion," says DeGroote, president and sole shareholder of Westbury International Corp., a full-service residential and commercial real estate developer.

"Then I like to see the building open and operate," adds DeGroote, 38, in an interview at his Burlington head office supported by a small, dedicated staff.

This start-to-finish approach is integral to the way DeGroote approaches business and life: He's a hands-on businessman who lives the experience, a developer who treats every venture as a personal project.

"I'd rather take on just one housing and two commercial projects at a time so I can maintain personal control and involvement," explains DeGroote.

"With this approach, I don't end up overextending myself - I'm always able to concentrate on making projects as successful as possible. I don't want to be the biggest developer - I just want to be a profitable company."

DeGroote founded his company in 1991 with a 238-unit condominium complex in London, Ontario.

His next project, closer to home, was the Roseland Green project on New Street, Burlington, a 145-unit condominium townhouse development.

This was soon followed by another Burlington development, Unsworth Green, with single-family homes on 41 lots he developed from raw land.

More recently, DeGroote embarked on the 216-unit condominium project Oaklands Green in Aldershot.

By the late 1990s, DeGroote had also undertaken four office buildings with 150,000 square feet on Winston Churchill Boulevard in Oakville.

He also holds land inventory for an additional 250,000 square feet of office space off the QEW in Oakville, which will become Westbury Office Park.

DeGroote also holds 37-acre and 47-acre properties near Burloak Drive that were to begin undergoing commercial development in 1999-2001.

Plans call for a 154-all-suites Westbury Hotel, over 400,000-square-feet of office space and over 1-million-square-feet of light industrial space.

> Founded on a growing reputation for excellence, his company has, by any measure, achieved a remarkable degree of success in less than a decade of business life."

"Every project gets all the personal attention it needs," DeGroote notes.

"We can concentrate on producing top quality, and since we don't take on more than we can handle, we're able to work through the market down cycles."

Some of DeGroote's success may be, if not genetic, certainly a family trait: His father is Michael G. DeGroote, a billionaire businessman with a strong influence on his youngest son's growing corporate prowess.

"One of the reasons I like to stay within my means, to not become over-leveraged or over-inventoried is my dad's influence," DeGroote notes. "He's always been there for advice and he's still my mentor in many things."

Another fatherly influence can be found in community involvement. While the senior DeGroote funds charitable groups and the Michael G. DeGroote School of Business at McMaster University, the youngest son oversees the school's entrepreneurs program. He's a big contributor to the Nelson Youth Centre and Burlington Community Development Corporation.

But while his famous father is there for support when needed, DeGroote owes much of his success to his own efforts and proven knack for building high-quality 'infill' developments.

DeGroote, who studied Business Administration at Sheridan College, had worked in the field operations of his father's former company, Laidlaw Inc., until the mid-1980s when he went to work for Toronto-based Cooper Construction for several years. While with Cooper, he developed a strong interest in real estate development.

In 1991, he founded Westbury International, borrowing the name from his father's Westbury Bermuda holding company.

"Dad has always been there for advice, but its mainly hands-off advice - he like us to do things for ourselves," explains DeGroote, youngest of four children, each of whom has fashioned success in their chosen endeavours.

From initial revenue of $2-million in 1991, Westbury International has experienced a tenfold increase in revenue, crossing the $20-million mark in 1998. Projections into the millennium call for continued growth. Profit, targeted to exceed 30 per cent of revenue, has been averaging 25 per cent, even through the past recession.

For entrepreneurs starting out, DeGroote advises taking a hands-on approach to business, staying within your means and never overextending yourself in financing or in the number or complexity of projects taken on.

DeGroote finds his self-financed, measured approach has earned his firm stability, even in economic downturns.

"And there's one other thing I believe is essential in achieving any success in life," he adds. "It's important to set priorities and live within them."

"I'm going at a comfortable pace I can live with. I'll continue in business for many years. I don't ever want to retire."

➢ *Michael H. DeGroote enjoys mapping out the future of Westbury International.*

Michael H. DeGroote

- Photo by Paul Sparrow

Enterprise 2000

Ron Joyce

Ron Joyce co-founded the entire Tim Hortons chain in Hamilton. But his first trip to the steel city was an unnerving experience that gave little indication of what lay ahead.

"It was a little scary," Joyce recalls. "It was also an exciting adventure. I had never been in any city until I got off the train at the CN station in Hamilton."

Joyce was barely 16 years old when he stepped off the train in 1947.

He had left a struggling economy in Nova Scotia and the little town of Tatamagouche for the promise of prosperity in Ontario's then-booming industrial heartland.

Although the names Ron Joyce and Tim Hortons are now inescapably linked to Hamilton, that first trip was an intimidating journey to a strange, sprawling city.

"I didn't know anyone in Hamilton, I didn't know the city at all and I didn't even know where I was going," Joyce recollects in an interview at his Jetport facility at Hamilton Airport.

"So I left the Hamilton CN station on James Street North and started walking south towards the downtown," Joyce continues.

"Then I decided to head west on Cannon Street where I came across a boarding house," he adds.

"I told the landlady I didn't have any money on me but I'd pay her board as soon as I got a job. She told me I had three days to get a job and pay her or I'd be back on the street. I moved in and shared a room with three men."

His landlady needn't have worried. The ambitious young man turned up the next day at the American Can company on Barton Street East, was immediately hired and started work that afternoon. Joyce would spend the next five years working at various factories in Hamilton, including International Harvester and Firestone.

In 1951, his adventurous spirit led Joyce to join the Royal Canadian Navy and serve in the Korean Conflict. He left the Navy in 1956 but would go on to serve another eight years in the Royal Canadian Navy Reserves.

"At that time, I had planned to make the Navy my career," Joyce recalls. "But there were other opportunities to consider back then."

> "I told the landlady I didn't have any money on me but I'd pay her board as soon as I got a job. She told me I had three days to get a job... or I'd be back on the street."

Joyce embraced one opportunity in 1956 when he returned to Hamilton and served the next nine years with the Hamilton Police force.

In 1963, his entrepreneurial spirit led him to buy a Dairy Queen franchise.

When he was unable to get a second DQ location, Joyce again looked at other opportunities in the marketplace.

He instead took over the first-ever Tim Hortons store in 1965. At the time, it was the only store owned by Horton, the legendary NHL Toronto Maple Leafs defenceman, who founded the Ottawa Street, Hamilton store in 1964.

"Tim and I developed quite a friendship," says Joyce, recalling his acquisition of the then-struggling store that still operates to this day.

By 1967, Joyce had opened two more stores and he and Horton became full partners. Joyce grew the business while Horton concentrated on his 25-year hockey career, mainly with the Leafs although he also played for the New York Rangers, Pittsburgh Penguins and Buffalo Sabres.

"Right from the start, our focus and our efforts were dedicated to becoming a successful franchise company," Joyce recollects. "We knew this was the best and fastest way to grow."

"We wanted to own as much of the real estate as possible – to control our own destiny," recalls Joyce who got his pilot's license after Tim Hortons expanded to Cornwall. He now flies a seaplane and Lear jet from Jetport.

Horton died in a 1974 car accident. After Horton's death, Joyce bought his shares and became sole owner of the chain that then numbered 40 stores.

By 1999, the Tim Hortons chain had revenue of $1.6 billion and 1,800 stores and kiosks, some serving communities as small as 3,000 people.

Tim Hortons was on target to reach its milestone 2,000th store by 2000, a year in which sales are also expected to reach the $2 billion mark for the Tim Hortons chain alone.

Under Joyce's leadership, Tim Hortons has grown to become the biggest coffee and donuts chain in Canada with 52 per cent of the market.

"We're very proud of the franchise operators who have played a major role in helping the company grow," says Joyce, the Senior Chairman of TDL (Tim Donut Limited) Group, the Oakville-based licensing company for Tim Hortons franchises.

Joyce also initiated and drove both the combo concept and the 1995 merger with Ohio-based Wendy's, the world's third-largest fast-food chain with some 5,000 restaurants.

The merged firm has annual revenue of $7.5 billion US of which Hortons accounts for around $1 billion US.

Joyce is the largest shareholder of the merged firm and is good friends with Wendy's founder Dave Thomas.

"We can still grow," Joyce asserts.

"And we'll continue increasing the number of stores for years to come."

> ➢ Ron Joyce is set to explore new business horizons

Ron Joyce

- Photo by Paul Sparrow

Enterprise 2000

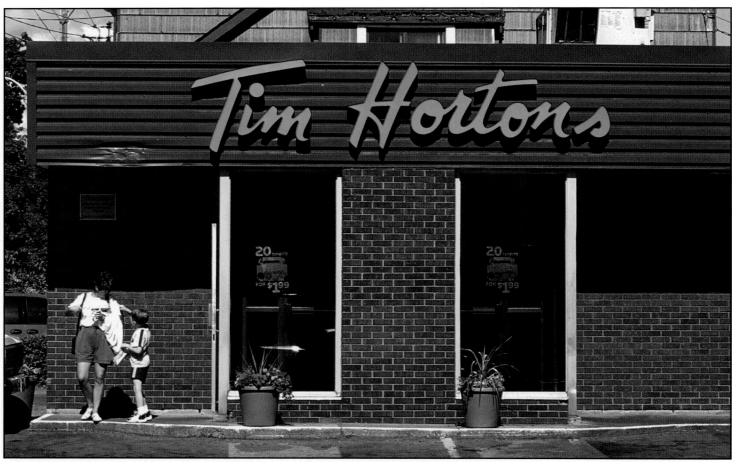

Taking a break at the original Tim Hortons store on Ottawa Street, Hamilton.   *- Photo by Paul Sparrow*

Tim Hortons is a fast food empire that continues to steadily expand.

By 1999, there were more than 100 Tim Hortons and Wendy's combo restaurants plus 35 in development.

All of this growth is literally feeding a seemingly insatiable public appetite for great coffee, soups and baked goods at Tim Hortons; tasty hamburgers, salads and stuffed pita sandwiches at Wendy's.

But Tim Hortons co-founder Ron Joyce is also expanding his horizons beyond a successful fast food business.

In the fall of 1999, Joyce opened a 1,000-acre resort in Nova Scotia with a marina and 5,000-foot runway to accommodate fly-in vacationers eager to fish, hunt or simply enjoy the resort peninsula's scenic splendour. Guests can also enjoy tennis courts or golf on a professionally designed golf course.

He's also owner of the NHL Calgary Flames and has residences in Calgary, Burlington, Florida and Nova Scotia.

And there's his 40,000-square-foot Jetport facility at Hamilton Airport to meet the travel needs of executives.

"My focus is still on Tim Hortons," Joyce smiles reassuringly when asked of his diversified interests. "And the Hamilton-Halton area is still where I centralize my business activities."

In Tim Horton's honour, Joyce established the Tim Horton Children's Foundation, a non-profit charitable organization that runs summer camps for under-privileged children. The camps are located at Tatamagouche, Nova Scotia; Parry Sound, Ontario; Kananaskis County, Alberta; and Quvon, Quebec in Canada. New camps are to open in 2001 at St. George, Ontario and Kentucky.

His tireless charitable work as chairman of the foundation earned Joyce the 1991 Gary Wright Humanitarian Award – and a 1992 appointment to the Order of Canada.

He has been named a Fellow of the

Hostelry Institute and has earned the Ontario Hostelry Institute Gold Award as Chain Restaurant Operator of 1992.

Joyce has also received a Honourary Doctorate of Commerce from St. Mary's University at Halifax and the McGill University Management Achievement Award.

In the late 1990s, he also received Honourary Doctorate degrees from Mount Allison University in Sackville, New Brunswick, McMaster University in Hamilton and Queen's University in Kingston. He's been inducted in the Nova Scotia Business Hall of Fame. He's also received the Canadian Franchise Association's Lifetime Achievement Award.

In early 1999, he was inducted into the Canadian Business Hall of Fame.

And In the late 1990s, after Joyce provided a generous donation, Hamilton Place was renamed the Ronald V. Joyce Centre for The Performing Arts at Hamilton Place.

Enterprise 2000

SERVICE PROVIDERS

Is there anything more important than great service? It's become a standard by which we measure others and ourselves. It's the cornerstone of every successful business. It literally drives the economy.

In fact, the rapid rise of the so-called service sector has made one thing very clear: The catchall 'service sector' phrase is outdated: There are now many service-oriented sectors accounting for over half the Canadian economy.

When manufacturing completely dominated the economy, it was convenient to dismiss any non-manufacturing activity as being part of the service sector. Now, services are growing much faster than manufacturing and their importance to our economic health cannot be dismissed.

The growth of services is fueled by a growing trend towards specialization, offers Lee Kirkby, the former executive director of the Hamilton & District Chamber of Commerce.

"You'll often find the most individual-focused employment is in the service fields," says Kirkby, "because that's where personal expertise is being bought and sold."

"The rising number of consulting jobs, computer experts and technical experts is evidence of a growing demand for certain types of service expertise in today's marketplace," he adds.

"It's all part of a fundamental shift on our economy," Kirkby continues. "Information and knowledge are more important now than ever before."

"And people who can offer services related to information and knowledge are clearly in demand," concludes Kirkby who is now a vice-president at Leppert Business Systems Inc.

Kirkby notes Leppert Business Systems has shifted, from being primarily an office products retailer that threw in services for free, to being primarily a services-oriented firm.

We'll learn more about LBS in upcoming pages.

We'll also learn about Market Matters, an enterprising marketing firm that excels at providing great services and expert consultations to a growing list of major clients.

Another company given profile treatment is Beverly Tire, a diversified firm that also emphasizes its array of services.

And we welcome back Dr. Roland Estrabillo, an innovative dentist featured in my last book, Success Stories. This time, Estrabillo shares his fascinating, life-changing experience swimming with dolphins. It's a truly inspiring story.

All of these companies and individuals, and others cited throughout this book, can be reached via the directory at the back of this book by anyone wanting additional information.

Meanwhile, you find out a great deal more about these inspirational companies by reading their featured profiles.

Their stories appear next.

Market Matters

Trishia Roque believes every client company is a specialist in their sector with distinct strengths that set them apart from rivals.

And Roque, president of Hamilton-based Market Matters Inc., delights in uncovering these often-hidden attributes of clients.

She also believes in finding creative, effective ways to promote these special qualities to ultimately improve a client firm's profitability. Roque has a proven knack for encapsulating and reflecting a company's unique personality in media presentations.

Most importantly, Roque believes in fulfilling her marketer's role while applying solid Christian ethics of honesty, integrity and fair play.

All of these beliefs are at the core of a Market Matters value system that establishes that everyone the company deals with has the right to feel they're understood and appreciated.

And this value system is the driving force motivating Roque and her company. It's what they're all about.

Roque and her company get to know their clients, assess their strengths and develop a marketing campaign that best suits the client's needs.

"We create for our clients a distinctive profile in the marketplace," Roque explains in an interview at the company's Goderich Road headquarters in east Hamilton.

That profile, she elaborates, involves "conveying a persona that defines the philosophy, values and integrity of our client's product or service."

"Every client is different – therefore, every campaign must be tailored to meet his or her specific needs," she adds. "If one doesn't have a well-organized, professionally tailored strategy in place, you're not taking full advantage of marketing opportunities. Planning is vital and we take a well-planned approach."

That approach has generated considerable success and recognition for clients and Market Matters.

Roque has won numerous awards recognizing her excellence in service and performance. These include the Press Awards for Canada recognizing her work in creating effective advertising. She did everything from writing copy to choosing graphics and controlling layout/finished ad.

Roque was once named to Chatelaine magazine's list of top Canadian businesswomen. More recently, she was awarded a Canada-wide advertising campaign for a national non-profit organization.

"We create for our clients a distinctive profile in the marketplace… conveying a persona that defines the philosophy, values and integrity of our client's product or service."

As well, CNN has selected Market Matters as one of just two firms in Canada for advertising, marketing and communication services for CNN's corporate clients utilizing the media giant's information network.

Under the agreement, CNN refers clients from anywhere in the world to Market Matters when they need advertising and marketing services aimed at the Canadian market.

"It's very gratifying to know that if a CNN client company from Germany or anywhere else in Europe or the world wants to do business in Canada, they'll be referred to us for their marketing needs," Roque notes.

She's also been approached by a consulate general's office to work with diplomats and consulate staff to develop their relationship-building and communication skills. She's a sought-after motivational speaker and frequent guest on radio shows.

Market Matters was also chosen to provide all the creative and promotional services required for the International Children's Games being held in Hamilton in 2000. With 23 nations participating, the Games provide an early look at many of tomorrow's Olympic athletes.

Add to these accolades and distinctions a client list that reads like a virtual Who's Who of prominent companies and you have an astonishing success story for a company founded in 1998.

Roque's personal marketing roots run deeper. In the 1980s, she and her former husband ran a multi-million-dollar real estate building and development firm where she earned many sales and marketing awards.

In 1997, with over 20 years of marketing experience, Roque founded The Headway Group, an umbrella firm housing Market Matters and her award-winning interior design firm.

"Of my companies, Market Matters has come to the forefront," she notes.

Roque takes a genuine interest in client needs while "honouring the execution of performance and honouring life through the application of how we live and what we do every day."

In addition to preparing marketing plans, her company also provides exposure through trade shows, web sites, direct mail, advertising, logos, press releases and media events.

With a warm and friendly manner, Roque has a knack for developing the right marketing strategy.

"Don't be surprised," she says with a smile, "if our recommendations result in you spending less money to achieve greater results."

> ➤ *Award-winning Trishia Roque takes an honoured position of service towards her clients.*

Market Matters

Dr. Roland Estrabillo

The dolphins came splashing towards him, leaping through the water with unbridled joy.

As Dr. Roland Estrabillo stood in the water off a beach in Hawaii, the dolphins danced into the sheltered cove, chattering excitedly. They seemed to be beckoning the Hamilton dentist to join them.

"I had been looking in the water at brightly coloured fish when dolphins suddenly appeared," Estrabillo recalls in an interview at his Upper Wentworth Street offices.

"They seemed so joyful, playful," he adds, "and I was fascinated by them."

Estrabillo swam up to the dolphins.

"As I moved closer, they started swimming around me – they wanted to play," he recollects with a smile.

"I began following them, swimming with them, sometimes holding on to them and letting them pull me through the water – it was wonderful," he says.

"They have such a joyful attitude – wouldn't it be nice if you could be as happy as a dolphin in life," Estrabillo adds, "and I love their sense of freedom, confidence and happiness."

"It was an experience I'll never forget," he says of the 1989 encounter.

Inspired by the dolphins, Estrabillo placed likenesses of their happy images on his business cards. As well, he's decorated the walls of his office with illustrations of dolphins at play.

He's also infused himself and his staff with a contagious dolphin-like, happy, confident attitude that puts patients at ease and makes trips to the dentist more enjoyable.

That Estrabillo would learn from dolphins and apply those lessons to his practice isn't surprising. This dentist believes in lifelong learning and has long selected mentors from dentistry and other fields to give him guidance.

Estrabillo is determined to keep up in the fast evolving field of dentistry.

He attends many monthly seminars and invests in computer equipment; technology, methodologies and materials to ensure his practice can treat patients fast and efficiently.

For example, his I-V sedation certification means he can comfortably sedate patients for longer periods while he performs cosmetic dentistry or full-mouth reconstructive surgery.

Although general family dentistry still accounted for 60 per cent of his practice in the mid-1990s, Estrabillo was concentrating more on full-mouth reconstructive dentistry as a growing, satisfying, part of his work.

> "They have such a joyful attitude – wouldn't it be nice if you could be as happy as a dolphin in life… I love their sense of freedom, confidence and happiness."

"After the orthodontist and periodontist have treated the patient, I perform bridge work, teeth implants, crowns, veneers and cosmetic improvements to teeth," he explains.

"We've cut the time needed for a crown to half an hour from an hour, so the patient is more comfortable."

Dr. Estrabillo now takes two hours instead of seven to perform most full-mouth reconstruction procedures. He notes this dentistry can improve chewing efficiency, improve the functioning of the jaw, save teeth and "actually make people look younger with whiter, rearranged, straighter teeth which support the mouth better."

He's also determined to make his office, himself and his entire staff as financially successful as possible. As profits exceed target levels, the staff receives a share of the surplus to spend or invest as they please.

Estrabillo also shares the knowledge he's learned, hosting regular seminars to impart product and methodology information to other dentists.

His wife Maria operates her own off-site laboratory where she performs lab work for more complex crowns bridges and veneers.

Estrabillo arrived in Canada from the Philippines in 1980 at age 20.

After graduating in 1987 from the University of Toronto with a degree in dentistry, Estrabillo set up practice on Upper Wentworth Street in a strip mall opposite Lime Ridge Mall.

Building his practice from scratch, Estrabillo had over 10,000 mainly active patients by the late 1990s.

By the early 1990s, he outgrew his mall location and moved to renovated offices at his former home, also on Upper Wentworth. After expanding the number of operating rooms to seven from four, he's now contemplating moving to larger offices in Hamilton to serve his growing practice.

Fuelling this impressive growth are referrals from satisfied patients who appreciate the extra care Estrabillo takes to make visits pleasant and brief.

And he's grateful for the input, advice and support he's received from his mentors, fellow dentists, staff and friends from all walks of life who have helped him overcome problems and achieve new levels of success in a demanding, time-consuming career.

"Success is never something you achieve all by yourself. It's when learn from others and share your own experiences that you improve in the process. And everyone benefits from this type of sharing."

Estrabillo attributes much of the success of his busy practice to his staff of 16, including a hygienist, support staff, and three other dentists.

"My staff is great. Without them I couldn't succeed. We do the best job we can - and we try to have fun in the process. We really enjoy our work."

> ➢ *Dr. Roland Estrabillo has adopted the confident, joyful attitude of dolphins at his dental practice.*

Dr. Roland Estrabillo

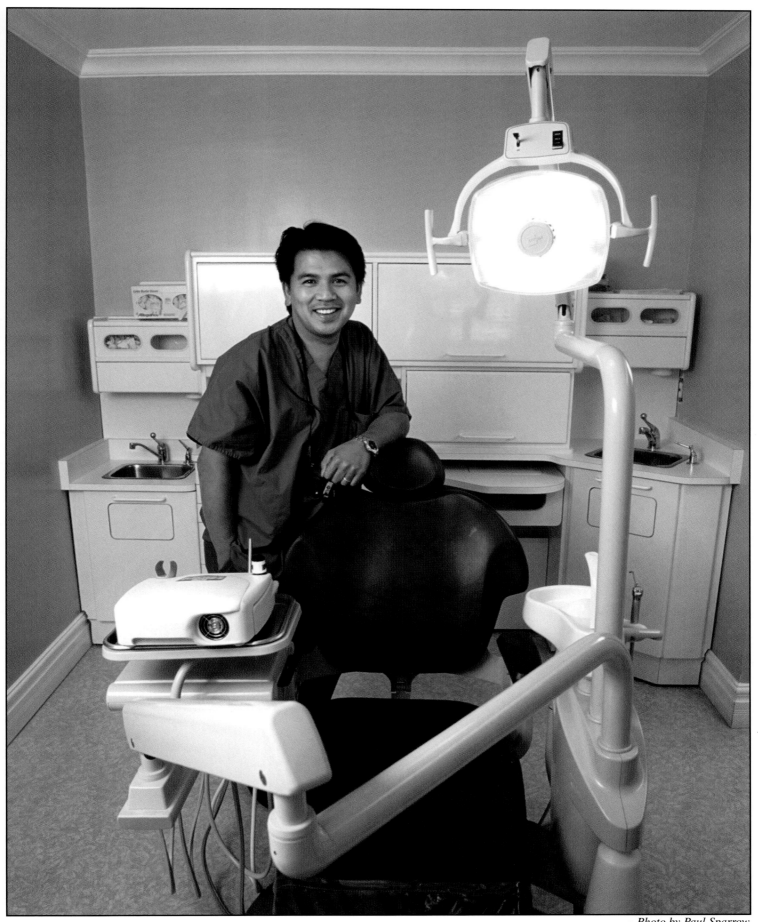

- Photo by Paul Sparrow

Enterprise 2000

Beverly Tire

It's now one of Canada's fastest-growing firms. But Beverly Tire continues to focus on the communities and people it serves.

"Community involvement is a large part of why we're successful at Beverly Tire," notes President Bill Farmer, "and it always will be a big part of what we do."

Farmer says the firm continues to focus sharply on customer satisfaction, bringing out the best in its own people and contributing to the well being of every community it locates in.

Jim Bethune, senior vice-president, notes the values Farmer describes are core to the way Beverly Tire operates.

"Our commitment to our customers, our people and our communities is really what we're all about," adds Bethune in an interview at the firm's head office in the Waterdown area, north of Clappison's Corners.

Kerry O'Brien Langford, vice-president of marketing and communications, nods in agreement.

"Flamborough is where we began and we're still very involved in that community," she notes. "We get involved in local fairs, charity golf tournaments, youth sports teams and service clubs."

While some companies restrict their community involvement to their head office town or city, Beverly Tire plays an active role in every community where it has a location.

"We'll continue to be involved in the communities we grow into," Langford asserts. The firm celebrated 25 years in business in 1999.

"Beverly Tire has never lost the local touch," she notes, "even though we're

experiencing a great deal of growth."

The firm is indeed growing steadily as it enters the new millennium. And it has a history of growth.

Founded in 1974 in Flamborough's Beverly community, Beverly Tire was a small operation when Farmer acquired the firm in 1980.

Under Farmer's leadership, the company began growing. In 1985 it moved to a 12,000-square-foot location in Waterdown and entered the retail tire business.

By 1989, Beverly Tire started from Waterdown OTR (off the road) tire and service operations plus a retail and commercial outlet in Stoney Creek.

"We'll continue to be involved in the communities we grow into… Beverly Tire has never lost the local touch even though we're experiencing a lot of growth."

During the early 1990s, the company bought its first retail-only outlet in Dundas, moved its OTR tire and service operations to Aberfoyle, bought a retail location on Hamilton Mountain and expanded retail automotive operations in all Hamilton area locations to include auto repairs.

In the mid-1990s, the company acquired The Dedicated Tire Company Limited in Orillia from Keith Kitchen who remains part owner of the location.

It also acquired Guelph Service Tire Limited from Richard Edwards who remains part owner of this location. And it bought Bolton Tire Sales and Retreaders from Ramiro Moniz and Oscar Moniz who remain as managers and co-owners of this location.

By this point, Profit Magazine had named Beverly Tire as one of the fastest growing companies in Canada. The firm also became a finalist as one of The Financial Post's 50 best-managed companies in Canada.

Acquisitions continued through the late 1990s. The company acquired Doyle's Auto Service locations in

Ancaster and Hamilton, the Hamilton and Burlington franchising rights of Thrifty Car Rental, Lynfair Tire in Brantford, Tires Only and Concorde Tire and Service, a commercial dealer.

And in 1999, the company signed an agreement in which Goodyear Canada purchased 49 per cent of Beverly Tire.

Seven more retail outlets opened in Guelph, Kitchener, Cambridge, Waterloo and Stoney Creek.

By that time, Beverly Tire had grown to include 200 employees and 19 successful commercial, OTR, retread, and retail tire outlets. It's the largest tire dealer in Hamilton and one of the largest in Ontario.

"The partnership with Goodyear makes good business sense for our customers and staff," notes Farmer.

"Our management team was interested in creating an alliance with a company that not only offers excellent products and services, but also has similar values and integrity. We found these qualities at Goodyear," he adds.

Farmer says Goodyear offers strong marketing support in advertising and promotions, plus extensive product knowledge, training and the ability to offer Air Miles reward miles.

"We have challenging objectives to reach and this partnership offers the support we need to make our long-held vision become a reality," he adds.

Bethune says the company will continue to grow in a managed way.

"You need great people to grow – we're fortunate to have highly skilled and motivated people," he says.

"We intend to keep growing while focusing on our people, our customer service and our community service."

➤ *Bill Farmer with store owners Hugh Thomson (Flamborough), Tony Doyle (Parkdale), and Scott McCartney (Mohawk Rd.)*

Beverly Tire

- *Photo by Paul Sparrow*

Enterprise 2000

Leppert Business Systems

It's a technological jungle out there. Searching the thickets for solutions can be an exercise in futility.

And it's easy to wind up lost. Many firms, immersed in the day-to-day challenges of running a business, lack the time or expertise to assess what technology is truly best suited to their needs.

They need a navigator to guide them through the maze. A growing number of firms are finding that navigator in Leppert Business Systems Inc.

"We research a client's needs and find solutions," explains Ian Leppert, president of the Hamilton-Burlington area firm that celebrates its 25th anniversary in 2000.

"And we help the business world's network widows and orphans – the firms who have been abandoned by a technology supplier who has either gone out of business or is no longer providing support," Leppert adds in an interview at the LBS head office.

"It's vitally important for any firm to be able to get the maximum benefit from their existing technology – or get matched up with a better system."

Lee Kirkby, company vice-president, nods in agreement.

"Understanding how a given firm wants to deploy the technology is key," Kirkby points out. "The technology is more complex now."

"A copier isn't just a copier anymore," he notes. "It can be an office tool that serves as a printer, copier, collator, document finisher and assembler, scanner and fax machine."

"You can also network this office tool to every employee's personal computer," he adds. "They can print, fax and put together documents without leaving their work station."

Companies also want to avoid spending time and money on overly complex technology they may not need. But for many companies, the primary problem is finding how they can harness technology to improve office productivity and efficiency.

And for many business managers, finding that right technological fit is a daunting task.

"It's vitally important for any firm to be able to get the maximum benefit from their existing technology – or get matched up with a better system."

Kirkby takes a methodical approach toward finding the right fit for clients.

"We have to understand their needs, get a sense of how paper flows through their office, get a clear understanding of how their business operates before we can determine the best solution."

"There's a certain amount of investigative work involved," Leppert concurs. "Clients aren't always able to effectively convey what they want or need so you look into it. You have to be a good detective in this business."

The company's business, as Leppert defines it, is now centred heavily on support services and consulting work.

"Leppert Business Systems specializes in providing technology solutions which assist clients with increasing their office productivity - and consulting services are now a big part of what we do," he adds.

It wasn't always that way.

The company's roots actually date back to 1936 with the founding of Herb Blake Office Machines.

Blake sold the business in 1975 to Leppert's parents, Peggy and Richard Leppert, who built up the business over the following decades.

Richard Leppert, who remains an active director and senior advisor at the company, took the business from its typewriter sales and repairs origins and transformed it, taking it to its next phase as an office equipment retailer.

Both Richard and Ian Leppert then took the company through its next stage of evolution, one introducing computers to the product mix.

Now Ian Leppert is steering the company into its latest stage, one more fully dominated by services, including consulting work.

"Before we sold the hardware and threw in the service," Leppert notes.

"But now, we sell the service more than the hardware."

Indeed, Leppert Business Systems has evolved into a full line technology solutions firm, specializing in office productivity systems for the efficient generation, storage and retrieval of electronic and paper documents.

"We try to come up with a solution that meets the client's needs and saves them some money compared to the way they were doing things before," Leppert explains.

An example of this approach: The G. T. French paper company received word from Bell Canada that the computer connection to their warehouse would no longer be available in its current form in the year 2000. LBS provided a less-costly and more secure Internet connection linking the firm's two locations.

LBS also has an arrangement with PricewaterhouseCoopers to provide firms with DocuCapture, a complete document management solution in which thousands of pages of paper archives are securely stored on CDs.

In fact, making business offices as efficient and productive as possible is really what LBS is all about.

"We're still a vendor with products and services to sell," notes Kirkby.

"But solving problems is the biggest thing we do."

➤ *Ian Leppert and Lee Kirkby stand behind their product, a printer, copier, fax machine networked to computers.*

Leppert Business Systems

- Photo by Paul Sparrow

Enterprise 2000

The Hamilton Spectator has been serving a Greater Hamilton readership for more than 150 years.

The large, regional daily newspaper moved from its downtown location to Frid Street in the 1970s where it continues to provide a wealth of insightful investigative news stories, major features and human interest stories..

The Spectator has gone through a number of changes in recent years and is today owned by The Toronto Star.

The Spectator is a heavy contributor of news and feature stories to the Toronto Star Newspapers Group.

- All photos on this page by Paul Sparrow.

CHML proudly bills itself as Hamilton's Hometown Radio.

Firmly entrenched in the Steel City's identity, 900 CHML has established deep community roots.

The radio station reaches a wide audience with its mix of informative Hamilton-oriented talk show programming, news and easy listening music.

CHML also gives back to the community through a number of programs included the Christmas Tree of Hope.

With sister station CKDS FM, CHML is finding new generations of Hamilton-area listeners.

CHAM Radio is Hamilton's Country Radio, happily tapping into a growing contemporary audience eager to embrace the latest hits by New Country artists.

Shania Twain, George Fox, Blue Rodeo and Garth Brooks are among the many artists featured on the CHAM playlist.

After reinventing itself several times over the years, CHAM and its country music format are now part of a larger group of radio stations in Southern Ontario.

Another successful Hamilton radio station is CKOC. An extensive profile on CKOC closes off the Media Specialists chapter.

MEDIA SPECIALISTS

As the pace of business life moves ever more quickly, information is becoming an increasingly valuable commodity.

More than ever, we're subjects of the Information Age. Our ability to successfully function in this brave new world depends, in large part, on access to information.

Record-high stock market participation rates, unprecedented investment levels, floating exchange rates, open borders and a global economy have all served to place a premium on communication services.

These factors and others have also served to expand the media marketplace. Instead of the death of newspapers, as some had predicted, we're seeing growth in the numbers and size of newspapers. At the same time, we're also seeing revitalized radio stations and growing universe of TV channels along with an exploding number of Internet web sites. And there's a strong market for this book and many others.

When The National Post arrived to join The Globe & Mail (where I previously worked) as a national newspaper, The Toronto Star (where I now work) positioned itself as Ontario's newspaper. The Star invested in people, technology, colour and content and increased circulation despite The Post's presence.

Other newspapers followed suit, similarly improving their product and growing the print market. These papers include those purchased by The Star to create a Southern Ontario network of great newspapers.

One of The Star's newspapers, The Hamilton Spectator, was my journalistic home for 17 years. While there were plenty of changes during my years with The Spec, the rate of change seems to have accelerated in recent years and readers are now being treated to fatter papers filled with top local stories and those provided via The Star's considerable resources.

Newspapers are now often more than print media. In my position as a Toronto Star editor, I operate a news service for The Star's sister papers, provide Internet newscasts and file electronic newscasts on TSTV, The Star's cable TV station.

Radio station CHML has cultivated community ties to proudly bill itself as Hamilton's Hometown Radio. CHAM has adopted a successful country music format. And CKOC has a winning formula with the music most of us grew up with.

Television station ONtv has widened its market reach and GT Associates offers clients WorldSites Internet services.

Stirling Print-All is an established member of the media positioning itself to capture a larger market share.

And Paul Sparrow, an exceptional Hamilton photographer, takes a multi-media approach that includes most of the impressive photography throughout this book.

We'll read more about Sparrow, ONtv, CKOC, GT Associates and Stirling Print-All, next.

ONtv

Bryan Ellis walks by walls, an elevator and pillars – as he enters a world that doesn't exist.

The walls aren't real. Neither are the pillars or elevator. Yet as you watch Ellis on a television monitor, he appears to be in an ornately decorated, two-storey room.

But look away from the monitor to where Ellis is actually standing, and it's obvious he's in a blue studio, by a blue desk, in front of a blue wall that's covered by a blue grid.

All of the decorative trappings, even the elevator, are computer-generated using essentially the same technology utilized in movies such as Star Wars. Welcome to the virtual set at ONtv.

The Hamilton television station made broadcast history in the spring of 1999 when it used the virtual set during its supper hour newscast. The attractive, richly coloured, three-dimensional, two-storey virtual set has been used continuously since then.

"We wanted to present our news packages in an impactful and visually stimulating fashion," explains Ellis, the executive vice-president and general manager of ONtv.

"This compelling technology will allow us the opportunities to do that," he adds. "Virtual set technology will also permit us, over the short and long term, to 'house' more sets in the same space, without large construction or studio dislocation costs."

"In addition," Ellis points out, "this discipline will permit us to quickly refine our sets according to changing consumer and client needs."

Simply put, ONtv can change and 'build' sets without moving anything heavier than a computer mouse.

ONtv Integration Systems Project Leader John Jarrett says ONtv has gone from taking days to build a physical set to spending minutes on a virtual set. "Maximizing studio space and time, as well as crew and control time is a great advantage," Jarrett says.

"Space on a computer and hard drive are our only limitations," he adds.

News anchor Dan McLean finds the adjustment has been relatively easy.

"Other than being able to see myself blink for the first time because of the seven frame time delay," he chuckles, "and being forbidden to wear blue as it would confuse the computer, there aren't huge differences for me…"

Ellis also emphasizes that the virtual set is being used responsibly.

"We wanted to present our news packages in an impactful and visually stimulating fashion… This compelling technology will allow us the opportunities to do that."

"Upholding our commitment to delivering relevant news information in the comprehensive, honest and timely way is what this is about," he says.

"This new technology will enhance our ability to do just that."

Art Reitmayer, president and CEO of parent company WIC Television Ltd., also recognizes the need to harness technological advances.

"New technology is increasing our speed of life," notes Reitmayer who is also president and CEO of ONtv after replacing Jim Macdonald in 1999.

"Our clients need us to move faster, to have more access to … market research and to develop positive professional relationships with them," he adds. "We're up to the challenge."

Accepting challenges has been an ONtv tradition since its founding as CHCH TV in 1954 by Ken Soble.

"Lucky Channel 11" began broadcasting as a privately owned affiliate of the CBC Network.

In 1961, under Soble's leadership, CHCH disaffiliated from the network to become Canada's first independent television station. A short time later, Soble converted the former Kenmore Theatre on King Street West into TV11's Telecentre and began building up his TV station's presence.

In 1984, the station's historic headquarters, a stately 1840's mansion, was joined to a modern, high-tech facility allowing the station to bring its operations under one roof.

By the mid-1990s, the station had grown to around 170 employees, a broadcast centre; two microwave mobiles, three production studios and three TV production mobiles.

Key to the continued health and longevity of the former CHCH is its 1993 acquisition by WIC (Western International Communications Ltd.)

WIC encompasses WIC Television Ltd., which also owns stations in Victoria, Vancouver, Kelowna, Lethbridge, Red Deer, Calgary, Edmonton and Montreal.

In 1997, WIC established a number of rebroadcast transmitters to allow the Hamilton TV station to broadcast to Ottawa, London and northern Ontario.

With its expansion into new markets, the former CHCH changed its name to ONtv to reflect its larger role as an *Ontario* TV network now reaching 90% of the provincial population.

Indeed, while Hamiltonians proudly call ONtv their own, the signal is actually broadcast across Ontario and into remote communities across Canada including the high Arctic - via the Cancom satellite service. ONtv has a reach of close to 5 million viewers.

"Anticipating trends, keeping pace with advancements and sustaining our ability to be responsive and interactive are some of the ways we're planning for the future," notes Ellis.

"However, one irreplaceable constant remains: the people at ONtv. Without their drive, tenacity and imagination, we would not be where we are today, nor ready for what tomorrow holds."

➢ *Despite what the TV monitor shows, Bryan Ellis is virtually alone in an ONtv studio.*

ONtv

- *Photo by Paul Sparrow*

Enterprise 2000

Paul Sparrow

Paul Sparrow never expected to get bitten by the shutterbug. Many people are glad he did.

As a Hamilton Collegiate Institute Grade 13 student, Sparrow planned to later study engineering at McMaster University.

"My assumption back then was that I'd take engineering and perhaps get into electronic engineering systems as my father had for Westinghouse Canada," Sparrow recalls.

"Then I got my first camera – and that changed everything."

It was 1973. Sparrow had become involved in shooting pictures for the high school's yearbook.

He soon found he was spending far more time in the darkroom than on his academic studies at HCI.

"I really got bitten by the bug," Sparrow recollects, "and I found I love taking photographs, developing them and seeing the results."

"While I got good marks in sciences, photography became my passion," the award-winning photographer adds in an interview at his Hess Street, Hamilton, office and studio.

"I'd always wanted an artistic outlet – and photography filled that gap."

After working a year to raise funds to finance a post-secondary education, Sparrow enrolled in 1975 in the Photographic Arts Program at Ryerson Polytechnical Institute in Toronto.

While studying at Ryerson, Sparrow was also building a reputation for excellence as a freelance photographer.

In 1980 he moved to his current location in the heart of Hess Village where he founded Multi-Media Techniques.

By the mid-1980s, Sparrow changed the focus of his business to become known simply as Paul Sparrow, photographer.

He's now spent some 20 years providing a range of services from the same location, including commercial photography, video, CD Rom and Website design, freelance photography for publications and multiple image audio-visual presentations in which images are projected on a large screen with surround sound to create a dynamic sensory experience.

"I think multi-image, audio-visual presentations present one of the most exciting mediums to communicate on an emotional level with an audience," Sparrow asserts. "The audience makes a personal, emotion connection."

> "It's very satisfying to have my work draw an emotional response from a viewer whether the image is part of a large presentation or a single photograph… The audience makes a personal, emotional connection."

The Multi-media work has corporate applications: One of Sparrow's presentations, for Laidlaw Inc., showed several stages of recycling. Another presentation, for Hamilton Region Conservation Authority, had a sound track sung by the Bach Elgar Choir.

Other presentations, at business conferences, have been effective means to convey ideas and approaches.

He also presented a compelling slide show, for Corrections Canada, showing a number of still images that took the viewer through a prisoner's journey from sentencing to incarceration to a return to society.

Sparrow has also presented The Elegance Of An Image, his own artistic presentation, which premiered at the Art Gallery of Hamilton.

He's also collaborated with actor David Victor to present – to rave reviews – The Human Touch, a unique theatrical event in which Sparrow's images interacted with the actor.

"It's very satisfying to have my work draw an emotional response from a viewer whether the image is part of a large presentation or a single photograph," says Sparrow whose work has been featured in numerous photography exhibits and in Canadian Geographic magazine, The Hamilton Spectator, annual reports, specialty publications and books, including the one you're reading right now. His work was featured in Photo Life magazines 10th anniversary issue and his brochure photography won an ACE award.

Sparrow loves photography. Between contracted shoots, he often engages in scenic photography for his own satisfaction. The result is that he boasts one of Hamilton's largest collections of stock photographic images of the city and environs.

What also sets Sparrow apart from many photographers is his proven ability to effectively wed technology and artistic talent to create captivating and intriguing images.

While many photographers seem adverse to change, Sparrow embraces technology, using technological advancements as tools of photography.

"I got involved with computers because the ability to effectively and repeatedly manipulate images is much greater that anything you'll find in a darkroom where you'll spend hours working with chemicals," he explains.

"There are also things you can't do in a darkroom that you can easily do with a computer," adds Sparrow who has become a master at digital manipulation to create and enhance unforgettable photographic images.

"I think we'll see many more technological advancements in photography and more opportunity from the Internet to effectively present images and make them come to life."

> ➤ *Paul Sparrow appears with just a small sampling of his photographic images.*

Paul Sparrow

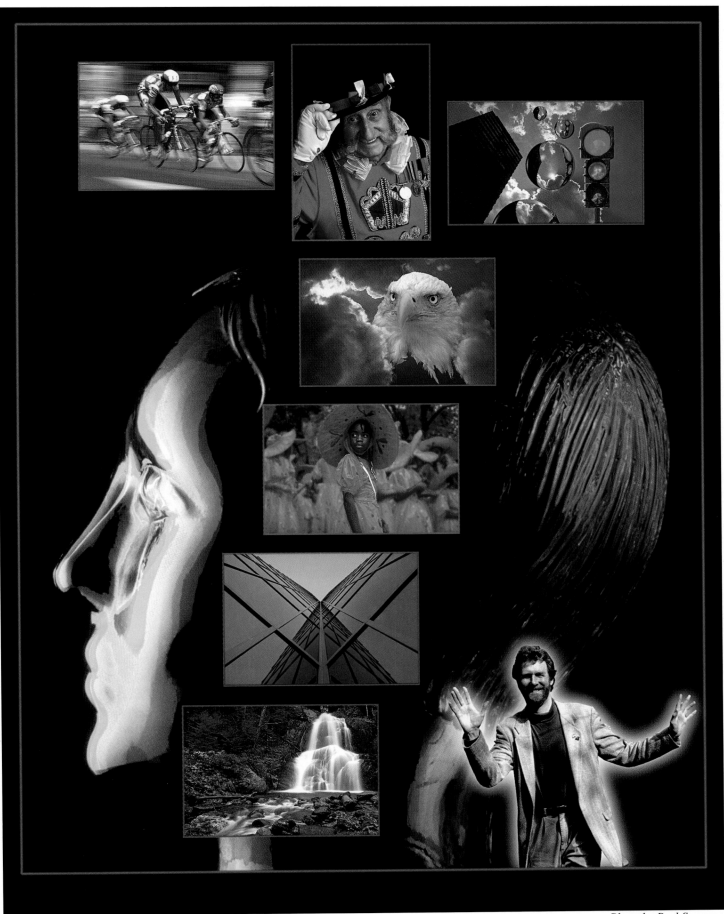

- *Photo by Paul Sparrow*

Enterprise 2000

Stirling Print-All

The death of print. The end of the written word. The paperless society.

Bob Stirling is pleased such dire predictions are proving groundless as we enter the new millennium.

The president of Hamilton-based Stirling Print-All has heard many doom-and-gloom forecasts through years of steady growth. He's been too busy expanding to pay much attention to warnings that the end is near.

His confidence is understandable: By 1999, Stirling was celebrating 25 years in business - with expectations that the firm's next quarter-century will be even more profitable than the first.

The death of print? Stirling simply doesn't buy it. He knows print will continue to be an important medium well into the 21st century.

"We still want to take comfort with a hard copy to rely on when a computer gets a virus or bug or crashes," notes Stirling in an interview at his King Street East plant and headquarters.

"We like to spend time reading hard copy information," he adds. "Reading a newspaper or brochure over a cup of coffee is relaxing and enjoyable. I don't foresee reading a newspaper on a laptop - that seems like work!"

Stirling takes no small satisfaction in the enduring vitality of print and paper.

"As a society, we're generating more paper now than we have in the past. So much for the paperless society!"

Yet Stirling is also acknowledges technological change and competing media have caused a contraction in the printing services industry.

This contraction was particularly bad news for less-astute former competitors who couldn't or wouldn't adapt to change and went under.

But Stirling survived and thrived, taking on the market share of displaced competitors and emerging as the leading area printer in a reduced and redefined market.

Stirling could have followed others who hid from the whirlwind of change and avoided risky expenditures on expensive new digital colour output services technology.

Instead, he invested heavily in the new technology, recognizing its potential for improving operations to provide better, faster service to clients.

> The gutsy move - which continues to pay impressive dividends - is the result of Stirling leading the industry and acting on a deeply ingrained business philosophy.

"Success often depends on openly embracing change, with all of its challenges," Stirling asserts. "You just have to look for the opportunities that exist in every challenge," he adds.

Stirling invested close to $1-million in digital technology. The investment that is expected to pay for itself over the next five years as demand for digital services continues to grow.

By the early 1990s, digital colour output services accounted for 10 % of Stirling's business. The lion's share was in traditional printing and binding.

As the year 2000 approached, about 30% of his business was digital as Stirling made greater use of the technology's ability to output full-colour images direct from disk to meet on-demand, just-in-time, black-and-white and full-colour services.

Stirling finds the digital colour output technology is ideal for addressing short-run demands for brochures, manuals, newsletters and catalogues. The firm can receive a customer's advertising prototype via computer, massage the information, provide imaging and send completed digital images back to the customer in a largely paperless creative process.

"Digital is very fast - virtually instant," says Stirling whose firm stands out in Greater Hamilton as a print shop and full graphic design shop that is also a digital/print super store.

"With digital, our initial proof is a usable copy and what you see is what you get, in living colour - or black-and-white," Stirling says with pride.

And he has decades of experience.

In the mid 1960s, he was a 16-year-old employee of hardware firm Wood Alexander when his hands first came in contact with printer's ink. He ran a a a printing press - and became immersed in the printing business.

Positions of press operator to branch manager of a print franchise followed.

Then, in 1974, Stirling went into business on his own, opening Stirling Print-All on King Street East.

By 1978, demand for services led his firm to move down King to its current location of King East at West Avenue, boasting 15,000 square feet of space.

In addition to technology, Stirling cites people as being vital to success.

Today, Stirling employs 38 people, including his wife Mary who oversees payroll; his assistant, Cathy Miller; his brother Bill, sales manager; Frank Fursman, plant manager; Ron Wilkie, creative director; comptroller Sandra Scaletta, credit manager James Case, copy services manager Valerie Clark, and sales associates Nancy Gamble, Wendy Stirling, Ian Wilkie, Jim Stahl, Kim Mallon and Jon Lazarowich.

The company now operates from 6 a.m. to 9 p.m., Monday to Friday. It's even open part-days on weekends.

Stirling catches his rivals napping by starting his workdays at 5 a.m.

As Fluke Transport President Ron Foxcroft notes, Stirling - named Man of the Year in 1998 by the Sertoma Club - supports many worthy causes.

"Bob Stirling is one of Hamilton's real heroes," notes Foxcroft, "and he's always there when citizens of this community need help."

➢ *Bob Stirling has conquered technology to deliver higher levels of service to customers.*

Stirling Print-All

- Photo by Paul Sparrow

Enterprise 2000

GT Associates

Experts say creating your own job and surfing the Internet may be necessary to succeed in tomorrow's computer-driven economy.

For Toby Young and Greg Brown, it's a case of "been there, done that." It's also a case of "still there, still doing that," as the two friends and business partners forge a role in the expanding cyber world.

Young and Brown are the new kids on the Web. They're partners in GT Associates, a diversified company with a WorldSites Network franchise at its core. Their franchise operation offers Internet marketing services to corporate clients.

"We get our clients found on the Internet," Young asserts as Brown nods in agreement during an interview at their Hamilton Mountain office.

"The client is listed in many different categories so a browser can type in any one of a number of categories and your name pops up," Young continues.

"We help you make the most of the Internet," he adds. "It's a very effective marketing tool because you find out where your customers and interested parties are and what they're most and least interested in knowing about you. But best of all, we make sure you're very easy to find."

Brown cites a real estate maxim when explaining why one of their sites offers superior benefits.

"It's location, location, location," he asserts. "We give you a prime location and promote it heavily. We also make sure your site has the look and feel of your company so you're represented as you should be and want to be."

The partners were selling websites

for $3,000 in 1999 and charging monthly maintenance fees of $50 on average. Sites can also changed and updated and e-commerce sites can also be set up for additional sums.

"Once you become our client," the hosting fees don't change," Brown notes. "The client gives us their input and we build them a custom site."

"We build your business on line through your custom website," Brown explains. "We grow with you. But we don't try to charge you more just because you're growing."

Young notes the client's website becomes a constant, effective promoter that reaches a mass audience and never sleeps. "As a client, you can just sit back and let your site work for you."

"It's a very effective marketing tool because you find out where your customers and interested parties are ... best of all, we make sure you're very easy to find."

"Your website with us becomes a 24-hour employee," Young continues, "and you know exactly how effective it is because we provide measurable results through the monthly reports we issue to all our clients."

These reports often contain more than 30 pages of statistics, setting out the number of times net surfers have "hit" or visited the client's site.

The reports also disclose which countries and regions the visitors are from and the amount of time actually spent visiting the client's site. Details are also provided concerning the most and least visited website pages so the client can get a sense of the popularity of pages and tailor the site accordingly.

Both friends say the connection with Mississauga-based WorldSites has been critical for their success.

"Tying in with an established, reputable, experienced company has really been key," Brown observes. "We can offer peace of mind to the client with the resources of a large company to support everything we do. It's all

about quality control – and the staff at WorldSites is second to none."

"If we went completely on our own, without WorldSites, we'd be another new business fatality," Young agrees. "This deal has helped us a lot."

In addition to the crucial WorldSites franchise, the partners also intend to eventually expand their business to include investments and interests in other companies.

"We're always looking for new opportunities to diversify," Young explains, "and that may one day include investments as silent partners in restaurants or night clubs, amusement parks and real estate."

Brown says the WorldSites franchise business also offers a window into potential investments.

"We learn a great deal about the firms we serve – so it's not too much of a stretch to see ourselves investing in some of them."

The two friends grew up together on Hamilton Mountain, shared a love for athletics and attended many of the same schools. After graduating from high school, they earned college diplomas and worked a number of jobs, with both ending up working at Hamilton International Airport.

Their story might have ended there, had they not noticed a WorldSites franchise advertisement in The Spectator and pursued this opportunity.

Borrowing money from family and friends, they acted on their long-held dream of starting their own business.

"I really have no regrets at all doing this," Brown asserts. "In fact, I'd regret it more if we didn't go into business."

"This is really what we want to do – and the future looks very promising," Young agrees.

"Besides, how many guys in their mid-twenties can say they're their own boss? How many can say they're making their dreams come true?"

➢ *Partners Toby Young and Greg Brown are the new kids on the Web.*

GT Associates

- *Photo by Paul Sparrow*

Enterprise 2000

CKOC/Y95

CKOC offers informative talk shows - and plays the music of our lives

- Photo by Paul Sparrow

They're playing our song. Two Hamilton radio stations have hit the demographic jackpot. Baby Boomers have a friend in CKOC and K-Lite FM.

Although both radio stations are also reaching out to younger audiences, CKOC's AM radio forte consists of the music we forty-somethings grew up with.

Sister FM station K-Lite FM leans to lighter, contemporary music that's soothing to rock concert-damaged ears.

They're serving up the music of our lives. And they've been playing our song for a very long time.

CKOC is Ontario's oldest radio station. It's second only to Montreal's CFCF as Canada's oldest station.

CKOC celebrated its 75th anniversary in 1997 and looks forward to toasting 80 years early in the new millennium.

Founded in 1922 by Herb Slack, CKOC inadvertently gave rise to a rival radio station in 1926, legend has it, when Slack pulled the plug on a First United Church broadcast which ventured into politics with a lecture on prohibition. The incensed parishioners formed Maple Leaf Broadcasting and started up CHML. In essence, Slack was the father of two radio stations in Hamilton. He's certainly the founding father of the Hamilton radio experience, as it was then, and is now.

The community pride and spirit Slack infused CKOC with continues to this day. It's a radio station that values its Hamilton roots and plays a vital role in the city's life.

As it was in Slack's day, CKOC's play list responds to a simple question: What do Hamiltonians want to hear?

But there's a great deal more to CKOC and K-Lite FM than a lot of great music: Newscasts, on-air banter and interviews are also part of both stations' successful listening mix.

For example, Bob Sherwin can be counted on for interesting on-air guests and informative interviews while he also spins some discs. Sherwin is the amiable on-air personality best known for his ongoing embrace of 1950s-1960s music under a time-honoured Oldies 1150 CKOC format.

And 102.9 K-Lite FM has the number one-ranked Sunni and Hayes show, with the upbeat duo of Sunni Genesco and Matt Hayes, who doubles as ONtv's light-hearted weatherman.

Both on-air hosts play an active, supportive role in the community.

And their fun-filled, on-air camaraderie can actually have you looking forward to getting up for work each morning. A morning smile is assured when you "turn on the Lite," and catch Sunni and Hayes.

THE NEW GENERATION

The ability of the new generation to create jobs and drive the economy is absolutely critical. How are today's young people being prepared for the challenges ahead?

That's the central question as many existing employers downsize workforces to cut costs and improve profits.

Although the number of jobs offered by large employers is shrinking, the demand for skilled positions is actually rising. As firms downsize, they strive to increase productivity via more automation along with multi-tasking by employees.

The trend to multi-tasking is creating demand for skilled positions as employers need people to perform an array of tasks. A simple labour job of the past is often combined with maintenance and other tasks, creating a hybrid skilled job.

In fact, the standard labour jobs of the past are disappearing, giving way to demand for multi-function skilled positions.

Computer literacy is also highly valued. Virtually all businesses depend on computers for at least part of their operation. Computers are essential, whether they're used to maintain customer files, track shipments and inventories, perform accounting, do design work or dispense information.

Here again, the emphasis is on marketable skills. Access to jobs is enhanced if you can run computer programs with ease.

And while large employers will continue to be an important source of jobs, small firms together employ more people.

Companies employing fewer than 100 employees already dominate the existing job market. Canada is rapidly evolving into a nation of small firms serving niche markets. The Canadian economy is now, largely, a small business economy.

Given reduced job opportunities by downsizing large employers, the ability to fit in with a small firm or create your own job has never been so overwhelmingly important.

Long gone are the days when anyone could graduate from high school and land a job with a big firm for life.

There is now a pressing need for graduates to clearly assess market opportunities, act on their dreams and create jobs for themselves and others in a new self-serve job market.

Most of people graduating early in the new millennium will work for companies that don't even exist today.

The New Age prizes innovative self-sufficiency. It's a create-your-own-job economy. To survive and thrive in this brave new world, it may well become necessary to take a do-it-yourself approach to jobs, assess your skill sets, fit them to market needs and start a business to serve marketplace demand.

"The trend is for home-based businesses to continue to grow and small businesses to maintain their role as the leading source of jobs in our economy," notes John Dolbec, executive director of the Hamilton & District Chamber of Commerce.

"Where you once needed an office with support staff to accomplish certain tasks, now an individual working from home on a computer can accomplish a great deal," he adds.

Dolbec says the ability of a home computer to quickly

The New Generation

Mohawk students are entering a brave new world of changing employment conditions. — *Photo by Paul Sparrow*

transmit information, faxes and documents marks a quantum leap in the capabilities of home-based firms.

"Small business is where our employment growth has been coming from and it's an incubator for future growth in jobs and business," he adds.

"After all, 82 per cent or more of the firms in Greater Hamilton have ten employees or less," Dolbec notes.

Neighbouring Halton region is also experiencing explosive growth in the sheer numbers of start-up small businesses and entrepreneurs.

"Only one private sector employer in Halton employs more than 1,000 people," Halton region's Economic Activity report observes.

There's no question entrepreneurs are driving the economy, creating many new jobs in the process.

We've already discussed what is being done at GHTEC and the Business Advisory Centre to kick-start young businesses already underway.

But let's return to our chapter's opening question: How are today's young people being prepared for the challenges that lie ahead?

Happily, there are many effective

answers to this central question.

At the high school level, career counseling and an emphasis on practical education, likely to lead to jobs, have both come to the forefront in many public schools.

And a number of private high schools are going even further.

Columbia International College takes a comprehensive approach to educating students who come to Hamilton for an education that will prepare them for a Canadian or American university.

Assistance is provided in everything from mastering the English language to handling finances and learning how to contend with essay writing, exams and other demands of universities.

Hillfield-Strathallan College offers small classroom sizes, more individual attention and a focus on creating skilled and caring citizens who are well prepared to embrace post-secondary education challenges with a great deal of confidence.

Headmaster Bill Boyer notes the Hillfield-Strathallan "encourages self-directed learning."

"One of our goals is to give our students a good, basic understanding

of how technology works and to keep as many opportunities open for them as we possibly can."

Boyer observes that student access to computer programs is sufficient enough to allow most students to either operate a given computer program or to adapt to the program fairly quickly.

At Appleby College, to further prepare students for the millennium, every classroom is wired for computers. All students are provided with IBM ThinkPad laptop computers.

"We were among the first schools in Canada to introduce laptop computers to the classroom," Appleby spokesman Ian Hamilton says, "and the familiarity with computers can only help our students when they enter university."

While the schools are playing a major role in preparing students for challenges ahead, young people are also getting a window on the business world through Junior Achievement.

In Hamilton, the JA program has enjoyed working partnerships with McMaster University and Mohawk College. About 60 local businesses provide volunteer consultants.

Carol Montag, president and CEO of

The New Generation

Mohawk President Catherine Rellinger and students face the future with confidence.   *- Photo by Paul Sparrow*

Junior Achievement of Hamilton, says the key to JA's success at reaching young people is the hands-on involvement of the participants.

At the post-secondary level, gearing programs at job opportunities has long been the forte of Mohawk College of Applied Arts & Technology.

"Getting people ready for changing employment opportunities is the main thing we do," says Mohawk President Catherine Rellinger, noting that there is today an increase in the numbers of people creating their own jobs.

Fortunately, Mohawk College has a history of taking innovative and imaginative approaches to making education and employment opportunities effectively mesh.

Another major area of innovation in the field of employment can be found

in Mohawk's long-established practice of bringing in business and industry executives to provide extremely practical classroom instruction.

Innovation is also part of the curriculum at Sheridan College, the prime choice for animation education in all of Canada, and one of the world's top three animation schools.

But Sheridan is known for more than animation. The college also features schools in Arts & Design, Community & Liberal Studies, Business, Science & Technology and Computing & Information Management.

The Michael G. DeGroote School of Business at McMaster University has opened an Education Trading Centre to help give students a practical education in how a stock market functions.

Bob Hodgson, public affairs director

for the business school says the facility "puts us on the leading edge as one of the first Canadian schools to do this."

The business school is living up to its motto: "Our graduates hit their career path running."

With their close ties to the business world, these various education institutions are well positioned to respond fast to marketplace changes.

The directory at the back of this book contains telephone numbers of the various institutions cited.

Upcoming pages also feature a great deal of useful information on Mohawk, the Michael G. DeGroote School of Business at McMaster, Sheridan, Appleby, Junior Achievement, Hillfield-Strathallan and Columbia.

Read all about them, next.

Junior Achievement

A burning candle: Symbol of faith and hope. And for some Mountain Secondary students, the candle also brings that elusive first job experience firms demand.

The Mountain Secondary students are eager participants in a hands-on business program hosted at their vocational school by Junior Achievement of Hamilton.

With advice from unpaid, volunteer consultants from the local business community, the students formed Wick-Ed, a Junior Achievement Company, which manufactures and sells bees wax candles to the consumer market.

Other Mountain Secondary students formed their own JA companies that produced and sold products ranging from stress balls to specialty candles and toiletries gift baskets.

All of these temporary companies fulfilled the JA mandate of providing their youthful business executives with the experience of operating a company; producing, marketing and selling products; and managing inventory, costs, revenue and consumer demand.

This true-to-life business experience has a way of bringing out hidden talents in student participants while helping them to believe in themselves.

"They're tasting success and it's giving them confidence," notes Lorne Evans, vice-principal of Mountain Secondary school.

Carol Montag, president and CEO of Junior Achievement of Hamilton, says the change in Mountain Secondary students was truly inspiring.

"One girl, who would barely talk to me when the program started, later became so enthusiastic she would wait at the classroom door to tell me about the packages of candles she had sold," Montag recalls with a smile.

"Their company, Wick-Ed, became so busy that they had two students working as quality control agents," she adds in an interview at JA of Hamilton offices at Lloyd D. Jackson Square.

"We've had similar experiences and successes with our JA programs at other schools – it really is an effective way to build an awareness and appreciation of business. I love watching the students' enthusiasm and self-confidence grow."

Montag notes there are some 4,000 student-participants in JA programs in Hamilton-Wentworth region. About 3,700 of the students are in 40 schools from Grade 6 through high school. The remaining 300 students take their programs at the JA offices and at a branch at the North Hamilton Community Health Centre.

"Young people, parents and teachers know experience is crucial to become workforce ready. At JA, we teach entrepreneurship. Our students can increase the likelihood of being hired or successfully creating their own job."

Another branch will open soon in Stoney Creek as JA reaches out to more potential participants than ever.

The participation rate was expected to swell to more than 5,000 children early in the millennium – a five-fold increase over 1,000 participants in 1987 when Montag joined JA.

Founded in 1919 in Springfield, Mass., JA began in Canada in 1955 and now boasts 700,000 participants every year. The movement attracts about 4 million children globally and is an independent, not-for-profit organization supported by business.

In Hamilton the JA program has enjoyed working partnerships with McMaster University and Mohawk College. About 60 local businesses provide volunteer consultants. These supporters include representatives from Stelco Inc. and Dofasco Inc.; Ron Foxcroft of Fluke Transport, John Skirving of Canadian Tire at Centre Mall, and Bob Stirling, of Stirling Print-All, to name but a few.

Past participants have also returned to volunteer their services. Jody Bertozzi of DOVE Marketing is a former JA participant who now gives back to JA.

"I'm lucky to work with some great business people and see the turnaround in the children," says Montag.

She notes JA of Hamilton's 11th annual Governor's Dinner was the local organization's most successful fund-raising event ever. Billionaire businessman Michel G. DeGroote was a major sponsor. Guest speakers were Tim Hortons co-founder Ron Joyce and Wendy's founder Dave Thomas.

Montag says the key to JA's success at reaching young people is the hands-on involvement of the participants.

'We provide the material, curriculum public speaking tips and concepts and the volunteer business people teach them to the students who basically put all of it into action," she explains.

"The students come up with the idea for a company and they sell shares to finance their business," she adds.

"They manufacture, market and sell a product. Then, after 26 weeks they liquidate the company and the investors are paid back. It really is experiential learning. The best way to learn anything is to actually do it."

Montag said the basic values driving JA are more relevant than ever before.

"More people will be self-employed in the new generation than in any generation preceding it," she notes, "and some experts say as many as one person in three will be self-employed."

"Young people, parents and teachers know experience is crucial to become workforce ready. At JA, we teach entrepreneurship. Our students can increase the likelihood of being hired or successfully creating their own job."

➤ *Carol Montag and Junior Achievement participants examine JA products.*

Junior Achievement

- *Photo by Paul Sparrow*

Mohawk College

Mohawk College's ability to prepare people for employment is today more crucial than ever before.

"Getting people ready for changing employment opportunities is the main thing we do," notes Catherine Rellinger, president of Mohawk College of Applied Arts & Technology.

The increased emphasis on employable skills is in large part a response to changing societal and employer needs, Rellinger explains.

"Gone are the days when most people attended college to get the skills needed to obtain the job they'd hold for the rest of their life," she observes in an interview at the college campus on Fennell Avenue West on Hamilton's West Mountain.

"We've seen a lot of employment upheaval, companies have downsized and many are still downsizing," notes Rellinger, a former teacher, Workers Compensation executive and child welfare administrator.

"And many employees are moving from one temporary contract job to another," adds Rellinger who also spent 12 years at Seneca College in progressively senior roles.

"At one time, years ago, our student population consisted almost entirely of high school graduates going on to post-secondary education," she notes.

"But it's different now. Increasingly, we're drawing our students from the life-long learning stream, we're seeing more and more displaced workers seeking new skills, and it's causing us to rethink how learning takes place."

With life-long job security a distant memory for many Canadians, with contract work becoming the norm and with growing numbers of people creating their own jobs and acquiring fresh skill sets for entirely new jobs, Mohawk faces a formidable task in preparing students for a challenging new millennium.

Fortunately, Mohawk College has a history taking innovative and imaginative approaches to making education and employment opportunities effectively mesh.

"This is a college that stands with pride on its history of innovation," Rellinger notes. "Mohawk, for example, was the first community college to offer co-op education programs tied to the private sector."

> "Increasingly, we're drawing our students from the life-long learning stream, we're seeing more and more displaced workers seeking new skills, and it's causing us to rethink how learning takes place."

Co-op terms continue to be offered at Mohawk, providing students and potential employers the chance to check each other out in the workplace.

Through co-op terms, students acquire meaningful, hands-on work experience. Some later work fulltime for their co-op job placement firm.

Another major area of innovation in the field of employment can be found in Mohawk's long-established practice of bringing in business and industry executives to provide extremely practical classroom instruction.

Mohawk has also played a pioneering role in forging links between academia and business worlds, jointly creating programs that prepare students for the very specific requirements of a given job.

Rellinger and others at the college are in regular contact with the business community through various forums, including the Industry and Education Council and the Hamilton and District Chamber of Commerce.

And she sees further changes ahead.

"To some extent with the Internet," she suggests, "we'll move towards the model of a virtual college without walls or structured time slots for some courses and some students.

The physical college will continue to exist and serve a purpose, but a virtual college functioning alongside it would have the ability to reach people in remote areas or those with little time to attend classes."

Rellinger says the college will also continue to focus on further improving the quality of the education and job training experience.

"We're an important part of economic development. We play a critical role in preparing a viable workforce vital for continued economic growth."

Fuller recognition of college education is another challenge facing Mohawk. Rellinger notes that progress is being made on this front with the recent signing of a protocol to mesh recognition of college and university curriculum to allow students to move from one institution to another and have their work recognized. There is also a new Mohawk/McMaster Institute For Applied Health Sciences at McMaster University and the future possibility the college may one day grant applied degrees.

"We also go into the workplace with our programs and teach business-designed courses to employees on site," Rellinger notes with pride.

"We're going to continue to find ways to stay at the forefront as an institution offering a practical education that can be applied directly to employment needs."

> ➢ *Catherine Rellinger is preparing Mohawk College for challenges that lay ahead in the new millennium.*

Mohawk College

- Photo by Paul Sparrow

Enterprise 2000

Hillfield-Strathallan College

A small gathering of Hillfield-Strathallan students closely examines an animal skeleton as Bill Boyer looks on.

Boyer, headmaster since 1995, is pleased with the intensity of the students' interest. Curiosity and a thirst for knowledge are welcome attributes at this private school on West Hamilton Mountain.

"We try to nurture each student's desire to learn," Boyer explains in an on-campus interview.

"And we encourage self-directed learning," he adds. "When our senior students leave here, most have become independent and in charge of their lives. They have the skills, knowledge, confidence and flexibility necessary to make informed choices."

In addition to the senior school accommodating students through high school grades, Hillfield-Strathallan also consists of a junior school housing grades 5-8; a primary school offering junior kindergarten to Grade 4; and, a Montessori school where children aged two-and-a-half to nine years learn through their senses at their own pace.

The first stage of an expansion program will establish a new, larger Montessori school in a newly built 28,000-square-foot building at the campus at Fennell Avenue West and Garth Street.

This stage also means that the building that previously housed the Montessori school will hold a fifth science lab and some classes while Hillfield-Strathallan completes a phase-out of Grade 13.

The Artsplex will also be expanded to hold a new music room and a larger, refurbished theatre. Campus parking will nearly double to 190 spots.

Stage Two of the expansion program includes renovation of the rest of the Artsplex, and of the old Montessori school building to accommodate additional classes.

The renovations will allow Hillfield-Strathallan to accommodate its 1,100-student population while shrinking class sizes to an average of 20 students from 23 in the junior school.

"Small class sizes are an attraction here," Boyer notes, "because it allows us to provide more individual attention to students."

Stage Three of the expansion isn't expected to be undertaken for a few years into the new millennium. It includes developing programs in the Ecological Resource Area, helping it complete a transition to a multi-purpose facility.

> "Children today have a much different future than anything their parents experienced… One of our goals is to give our students a good, basic understanding of how technology works…"

Boyer notes Hillfield-Strathallan has adopted a plan to dedicate resources to the development of technical literacy to prepare students for life beyond this school, whether it's at university, college or in the workforce.

"In developing technical literacy, we're primarily focused on computer literacy, but we also have two video-editing suites and we're looking at adding a recording studio in the music room," Boyer adds.

"Our students are connected to the Internet and students in our junior and senior schools have e-mail addresses."

Boyer says Hillfield-Strathallan is committed to preparing its students for the challenges that lay ahead in the new millennium.

"Children today have a much different future than anything their parents experienced," he notes.

"One of our goals is to give our students a good, basic understanding

of how technology works and to keep as many opportunities open for them as we possibly can."

Boyer observes that student access to computer programs is sufficient enough to allow most students to either operate a given computer program or to adapt to the program fairly quickly. The skills are also honed in business-related programs and in the production of a yearbook in hard copy and CD.

Students are also provided with non-secular readings at this interfaith school to develop their spirituality.

There are also many athletics programs at various grade levels.

In addition to helping shape students intellectually, artistically and athletically, Hillfield-Strathallan encourages students to take part in charitable fundraising events, food drives and other community causes.

"It's a critical characteristic of what we do here," Boyer explains.

"We encourage students to accept a certain degree of responsibility to our community and take part in voluntary actions to enhance the lives of those less fortunate than themselves. For example, our senior school students held a 30-hour famine event that raised over $6,000 to assist refugees in the Yugoslavian conflict."

Helping to mould tomorrow's caring citizens is a role Boyer clearly enjoys.

"I find the biggest source of satisfaction in my job is watching the students interacting with other students and witnessing their physical and intellectual growth," he smiles.

"We want to make sure the educational experience for our students is as enriched as possible on a sustainable basis – and we'll continue to pursue that goal well into the new millennium."

➤ *Hillfield-Strathallan students examine animal bones while Bill Boyer looks on.*

Hillfield-Strathallan College

- Photo by Paul Sparrow

Enterprise 2000

Columbia International College

Most students entering Columbia International College are strangers in a strange land, coping with culture shock and a language barrier.

But by the time they complete their studies at this private international high school, they're familiar with Canada's customs, fluent in English, and well prepared for the many academic and social challenges awaiting them.

In fact, they're so well prepared that virtually 100 per cent of Columbia graduates are placed in universities in Canada and the United States.

Due to the excellent caliber of Columbia's graduates, universities across North America are eager to attract them.

Each year, Columbia graduates are awarded scholarships to prestigious universities. As part of the unique University Partners program, some graduates receive scholarships specifically created for Columbia students.

Academic success stories have become routine at Columbia, which in 1999, celebrated its 20th anniversary.

Columbia now has 120 staff members and over 600 students.

As the Hamilton-based school has grown from its original six-room school building on Mohawk Road to its current location on Main Street West, excellence in education has always remained a top priority.

"We provide our students with pre-university training to prepare them for success at Canadian universities," notes Columbia principal Anna Shkolnik.

Shkolnik notes some international students may be familiar with a very different post-secondary education system in which it is difficult to gain entry to a university, but once accepted, unless they fail courses, students are able to graduate regardless of academic performance.

In contrast, at Canadian universities, students must maintain a minimum average to remain in their programs and graduate.

"In some cases, students can go directly from a foreign country to a Canadian university – but it's a culture shock and they may not be prepared to meet the demands of university academics," notes Shkolnik.

"We feel there are leadership qualities in everyone – our goal as a school is to work with our students to further develop those qualities."

"In some cases, they will not be able to graduate because they lack the basic skills needed for academic success," she adds in an interview at the West Hamilton school.

"We help students earn their Ontario Secondary School Diploma. We also help them develop English language proficiency, good study habits, academic skills, essay writing expertise, skills needed to prepare lab reports, and leadership abilities," Shkolnik elaborates.

"By the time they leave Columbia, our students are ready to excel at university," she adds.

"Eventually, our students become the professionals and leaders of their communities."

To ease the transition to a new culture and leave more time for academic work, Columbia offers its students a Total Care Education system.

The system provides a level of care comparable to what the student would receive at home with their parents.

Total Care Education includes housekeeping, meals, and 24-hour supervision at the school's on-campus boys' residence and off-campus girls' residence.

It also includes assistance with managing finances and banking, health insurance, school physicians and medical services, career and personal counseling and English and Math tutorials.

Parents sending their children to Columbia take comfort in the secure and caring environment created by the Total Care Education system.

The Leadership Enrichment And Development (L.E.A.D.) Program is one aspect of a Columbia education that appeals to both students and parents.

"Columbia students often come from families of entrepreneurs and business leaders," notes Columbia Executive Director Clement Chan.

"These parents want their children to get a well-rounded education that will successfully prepare them for the future," he adds.

Jill Simon-Sinclair, coordinator of the L.E.A.D. Program at Columbia, notes: "Academic achievement alone can no longer guarantee that a student will have a successful future."

"Students need an education that goes beyond the classroom walls to teach skills and offer experiences in many different aspects of life," Simon-Sinclair adds.

"Through our leadership training program, we are able to offer students a well-rounded education," she explains.

The L.E.A.D. Program prepares students by teaching and emphasizing leadership skills such as teamwork, morals and ethics, decision-making and conflict resolution.

Columbia students are required to devote time to personal development and leadership training in addition to their academic studies.

Students have opportunities to practice leadership skills by participating in clubs and playing sports.

Columbia International College

Columbia students can also volunteer their time to work as school and residence prefects. They also have the opportunity to participate in student government.

"We feel there are leadership qualities in everyone – our goal as a school is to work with our students to further develop those qualities," explains Simon-Sinclair.

"We realize that the students in our classes today will be the leaders of tomorrow."

The L.E.A.D. Program reinforces the importance of service learning.

"Ultimately, we want our students to be agents of change," asserts Simon-Sinclair.

"We want them to have a positive effect on their communities, whether the community is at Columbia, at university, in Canada or in their home country," she adds.

Columbia students are already making a difference to the Hamilton-Wentworth community.

"Our students do a lot of community service," notes Shkolnik.

"They volunteer at Ronald McDonald House, the Hamilton Health Sciences Corporation and local daycare facilities," she notes.

Chan agrees that student volunteer involvement is extensive.

"Our students also like to get involved in fundraising events for charities and victims of natural disasters," he notes.

A unique component of the L.E.A.D. Program is the leadership training offered at Columbia's Bark Lake campus and Outdoor Education Centre in northern Ontario's Haliburton Highlands.

Columbia students and staff often

Columbia students are enthusiastic about education. — *Photo by Paul Sparrow*

use the facility for intensive leadership programs.

The Bark Lake experience involves activities such as canoeing, hiking, archery, orienteering, high rope climbing and goal setting sessions.

"Our Bark Lake facility offers an outstanding leadership training experience," notes Simon-Sinclair.

"It gives students an opportunity to practice using the leadership skills they have learned in the school," she adds.

The great achievements of Columbia graduates speak volumes about the quality of this international high school.

The combination of the Total Care Education system, high academic standards, and the L.E.A.D. program is a recipe for success that may well be unparalleled anywhere in Ontario.

All of which makes for a well-rounded, thorough and thoughtful educational experience at a school that acts a bridge between very diverse cultures.

"Columbia is recognized as an excellent school by many universities," notes Shkolnik.

"Our graduates leave here well-prepared and many of them go on to excel at university."

Appleby College

Shaping students into caring citizens is an Appleby College tradition.

"We've long emphasized community service," Headmaster Guy McLean states with pride.

"The students frequently do volunteer work at local hospitals or foodbanks," notes McLean, headmaster of the private, university-preparation school in Oakville since the late 1980s.

In 1998, Appleby students were given the opportunity of engaging in volunteer work terms of two hours per day, five days per week.

"We've created a core group of volunteers for local agencies – and it's worked really well," McLean points out in an interview at his ivy-covered office in one of a dozen buildings set in a leafy, park-like campus along Lake Ontario's northern shoreline. Appleby began as a boy's school in 1911 before going coed in the early 1990s. The school now teaches Grade 7 to OAC.

"Our students also run a camp for inner city children from Toronto's Regency Park area, giving children a chance to go swimming and enjoy the outdoors," McLean adds, noting that plans were also underway to create camps for handicapped children.

"We also run camps in northern Ontario. The adults are there as resources and the students are trained to run the camps. We're interested in developing leadership skills."

The emphasis on community service and leadership is part of a broad program to develop well-educated and well-rounded citizens capable of making a meaningful contribution to society.

"Being bright alone isn't enough to succeed as an Appleby student," notes McLean.

"Students must not only be able academically to handle the high school program and want to go on to university, they must also want to contribute to the school and want to be in this environment." McLean also points out that potential students go through an application screening process and interview to determine their suitability for Appleby College.

"There's both a financial and emotional investment in the program," McLean explains. "The students really have to decide that they want to be here. It's a different life."

Compared with many public schools, Appleby College plays a bigger role in a student's life. School days start at 8 a.m. and tend to run late with extracurricular activities added on to full course loads.

> "Being bright alone isn't enough to succeed as an Appleby student… There's both a financial and emotional investment in the program. The students really have to decide they want to be here."

Evenings can also include rehearsals, practices, and remedial help and tutoring from easily accessible teachers and faculty members, 30 of whom reside on the 59-acre campus. Students also tend to take home a good deal of homework, and about 200 of the school's 560 students live on campus.

Add in community service work plus after-school and weekend events and there's often little spare time left over.

"It can be its own world here," McLean observes. "We keep our students busy with athletics, activities and academics. It's a demanding program but one that is ultimately very rewarding for our students."

At Appleby, participation in a broad range of activities is mandatory.

"The students must be involved in sports, arts, music and service," McLean states. "But they can choose which sports they'll take part in. For example, some students prefer athletic activities that are not team-based, such as rock climbing, tennis, swimming, cycling, running, aerobics or karate."

There is also choice within the field of arts and students are also required to attend the plays and art exhibitions of other students.

"Through participation in the arts, students are able to develop a critical eye, analytical abilities, a spirit of cooperation and team-building skills," McLean explains. "The arts are at least as effective as sports in developing solid underlying sets of values."

In their last two years of study, Appleby College students can choose to specialize in an area of interest.

"Our goal is to make the students well-rounded individuals, to give them a good, broad foundation," McLean explains. "But many reach a point where they want to specialize and that's healthy too."

To further prepare Appleby College students for the new millennium, every classroom is wired for computers and all students are being provided with IBM ThinkPad laptop computers, notes Ian Hamilton, Appleby's executive director of public affairs.

"We were among the first schools in Canada to introduce laptop computers to the classroom," Hamilton states with pride, "and the familiarity with computers can only help our students when they enter university."

McLean discloses that the placement rate of Appleby grads at universities "is virtually 100 per cent and I think that offers some reassurance that we're taking the right approach."

That approach, McLean adds, will continue to emphasize new technology while at the same time retaining as its foundation, the traditional values that have always been a part of Appleby.

"Our students will continue to benefit from a broad-based experience."

> ➤ *Appleby college students employ laptop computer technology in park-like surroundings.*

Appleby College

- Photo by Paul Sparrow

Enterprise 2000

Sheridan College

The Mask, Jurassic Park and Mulan were brought to life by Sheridan College animation grads.

But flickering images of animated characters provide just a glimpse into the world of imagination and education at Sheridan College.

"We're the prime choice for animation education in all of Canada, and one of the top three institutions in the world, for teaching animation," Sheridan communications director Ron Holgerson proudly states.

"There are Sheridan grads in virtually every major animation studio and our graduates are known for their skill and creativity," Holgerson notes. "But there's a great deal more to Sheridan College than animation alone," he adds in an interview at the Trafalgar Road Campus in Oakville.

Indeed. Sheridan College is actually composed of five prominent schools with the world-famous School of Animation, Arts & Design accounting for 25 per cent of the student body.

About 26 per cent of the students are enrolled in Community and Liberal Studies, while 25 per cent are enrolled in Business courses, 10 per cent are in Science & Technology programs and 14 per cent study at the Computing & Information Management school.

All told, 10,700 full-time students and 42,000 continuing education students are enrolled in 90 courses offered at the Trafalgar Road Campus with a nearby Skills Training Centre and at the William G. Davis Campus in Brampton with its new student centre.

Founded as a community college in 1967, Sheridan now draws about 60 per cent of its student body from beyond Halton and Peel regions.

"All of our schools offer outstanding programs and have achieved a great deal of success," Holgerson notes. "For example, a Business student recently won the prestigious Ontario Global Traders Award."

And there's more: Illustration students recently won two-thirds of the Applied Arts magazine annual awards. Glass studio students won top awards from the International Glass Art Society. Media Arts students and grads won six film and television awards.

There are also plans to establish a research tech park at the Trafalgar Road Campus where businesses would be invited to set up shop and pass on their expertise in practical, hands-on courses offering real-life experience.

"There are Sheridan grads in virtually every major animation studio and our graduates are known for their skill and creativity."

But Holgerson readily admits the animation school has long captured the public's imagination. Beyond the film characters already mentioned, Sheridan grads were behind The Mummy, A Bug's Life, Fly Away Home and Antz.

Graduate Steve Williams lent his talents to such films as Terminator 2, Jurassic Park and Spawn.

Fellow graduate James Straus is responsible for the animation in Dragonheart, while another grad, Dennis Turner was behind Twister's spectacular tornado visual effects.

Some of Sheridan's successful graduates return to the college as adjunct professors to teach master classes to new generations of promising young animators.

In addition to strong demand for their skills from south of the border, opportunities are also flourishing in Canada. Disney has opened a studio near Toronto and additional hiring by Nelvana also ensures at least some of the grads can live and work in Canada.

The film industry isn't the only beneficiary of Sheridan's animation expertise. A new project partnering Sheridan with The Hospital for Sick Children is developing a multimedia centre to provide interactive, animated health information resources to children and their families.

The Trafalgar Road Campus is in a park-like setting just five minutes north of downtown Oakville. In the fall of 1999, students also had the opportunity to live on campus in a new students' residence.

Walking through this sprawling campus, students can be found working on laptop computers, sketching life drawings, sculpting, glass-making, taking in some classroom instruction, or visiting the Art and Art History Centre that opened in the fall of 1999.

A well-appointed library adjoins a botanical gardens study area and a new Sheridan Centre for Animation and Emerging Technologies (SCAET) is slated to open in September 2000.

As well as Animation, SCAET will be home to the Journalism-New Media program, a new Telecommunications Centre and the Advanced Television and Film postgraduate program, which will focus on digital media production and post-production training.

SCAET sets the stage for Sheridan's new millennium role as a leader in applied research in new technologies.

Add in Sheridan's success in forging business and public partnerships, its emphasis on postgraduate programs and its undiminished commitment to excellence and it's easy to appreciate the college's confidence in meeting the challenges of the new millennium.

Sheridan President Sheldon Levy is understandably enthusiastic.

"Whether in animation or science and technology or another area of education, Sheridan offers a program designed to help you realize your career objectives," Levy notes. "It's simply a fabulous place to study."

➢ *Sheridan College is one of the top schools in the world for animation studies.*

- Photo by Paul Sparrow

Enterprise 2000

Michael G. DeGroote School of Business

The trading floor's digital display boards run up-to-the-minute stock market results. Banks of computer screens flash with data. But this isn't the TSE.

It's the Educational Trading Centre at the Michael G. DeGroote School of Business. It opened in 1999 at the school at McMaster University.

Tomorrow's leaders - already getting a business education with an entrepreneurial edge - are now being taught tricks of the trade.

The 1,000-square-foot facility is only the second simulated stock market trading floor in Canada, notes Bob Hodgson, public affairs director for the business school.

"It puts us on the leading edge as one of the first Canadian schools to do this," Hodgson adds with enthusiasm.

"Our students are being given a real advantage with this facility."

Hodgson believes the facility, part of the school's finance program, will help increase the skill levels and marketability of business school graduates seeking employment.

"Employers often say our grads roll up their sleeves and get right to work. We always strive to live up to our school motto: Our graduates hit their career path running."

John Siam, director of the new centre, notes the facility has drawn favourable reactions from Bay Street and the wider investment community.

Indeed, Reuters (Canada) is providing the centre with financial information. The Chicago Board of Trade, New York Stock Exchange, Toronto Stock Exchange and the other Canadian exchanges have waived their usual fees. Other stock markets are providing data at little or no cost at all.

"At the Educational Trading Centre,

students have access to real-time stock and financial information," Siam notes.

"They can learn how markets work and develop the skills demanded by today's volatile business environment."

Brian Shaw, managing director of CIBC World Markets and the centre's first trader-in-residence, agrees.

"This is an astounding opportunity for students who want a career in financial services and an educational experience in a real trading room environment," he asserts.

"Employers often say our grads roll up their sleeves and get right to work. We always strive to live up to our school motto: Our graduates hit their career path running."

The centre was made possible through grants from CIBC World Markets while the business school itself has received substantial support from the chief benefactor it's named for, businessman Michael DeGroote.

The school has long endeavored to instill its programs with a measure of DeGroote's risk-taking business savvy.

McMaster University itself has repeatedly been ranked by Maclean's magazine as the most innovative university in Canada.

Although McMaster may move into offering a diploma in risk management and trading at a future date, the centre already applies hands-on experiential work supporting the curriculum of finance, marketing, health services management and accounting courses.

The Michael G. DeGroote School of Business has also introduced a new electronic commerce stream into its MBA program, focusing on management and technological issues.

Another change at the business school, effective early in 2000, is the appointment of Dr. Vishwanath V. Baba as school dean.

The Michael G. DeGroote School of Business is the first business school in Canada to take its MBA program and offer it right on a client's premises.

The off-campus MBA program is currently available at Cambridge Memorial Hospital and Mastech/Quantum.

Clients are charged a fixed rate fee to have staff take MBA courses at work. Courses are also somewhat tailored to meet the needs of employers.

The school has also offered a continuing education program for middle to upper management in the business community designated as MVP (Managing with Vision and Proficiency). Courses deal with people management, finance and innovation.

The school's MINT (Management of Innovation & New Technology) Research Centre places an emphasis on practical research, says MINT director Chris Bart.

"Our main goal is to do research that matters into the management of innovation and new technology," says Bart, "and we want to be Canada's pre-eminent research centre."

By mid-1997, MINT had created an environment for collaborative and interdisciplinary research in the field of innovation management. MINT has produced over 90 papers, initiated 24 research projects and held a conference on innovative entrepreneurs. Bart enthusiastically hails the research centre as a success, in part because "very few people ever drop out."

The business school as a whole is similarly successful. Virtually 100% of the MBAs achieve job placement.

The school's list of success stories includes MBA Wayne Fox, vice chairman, treasury and balance sheet management, CIBC.

"In McMaster's MBA program," Fox recalls, "I learned a skill that is in huge demand by every business in every industry: The ability to solve problems in a disciplined and focused way."

➤ *Entering a brave new world at McMaster University's Michael G. DeGroote School of Business.*

Michael G. DeGroote School of Business

- Photo by Paul Sparrow

Enterprise 2000

University Hall

The past exists comfortably with the future at McMaster University. — *Photo by Paul Sparrow*

Enterprise 2000

CLOSING NOTES
Limitless Horizons

The future is frightening. It's also exciting, exhilarating, fascinating, filled with risk, adventure, surprises and opportunity.

I deem the new millennium frightening because it lacks the security and stability of the past.

The phrase 'job security' is today an oxymoron. If you've been reading this book cover-to-cover, you've likely concluded employment stability (another oxymoron), if it exists at all, is built on the shifting sands of market conditions.

Very few people today hold the same jobs all their lives. Some look back in envy at the job stability their parents enjoyed. In fact, as late as the mid-1960s, people often complained of being stuck in a rut at work with a secure but dull job. Today, many would love to be stuck in such a rut.

Instead, downsizing companies are shedding jobs at an alarming rate. Many available jobs call for highly specialized skills. Those fortunate enough to find employment often have to settle for short-term contract work with no fringe benefits. When the contract ends, they again experience the upheaval of having to look for work.

Workers who once frequently complained about their monotonous job can suddenly find themselves wishing they had their old jobs back as they wait on the unemployment line after many years with a given firm. The upheaval can be traumatic and leave the victims questioning their self-worth.

Yet this unsettling job loss can also present a time of great opportunity. It can provide the chance to start that business you've contemplated but never quite got around to because it was easier to simply show up at the same old job every day.

Losing a job can mean losing a comfortable crutch. It can leave you with a challenge to pursue the dreams you've long put on hold. Even if you don't start your own business, you may find work in another field that offers more personal satisfaction than your old job ever could.

Closing Notes: Limitless Horizons

Suddenly, your narrow little world expands. New, limitless horizons stretch before you and you have a new chance to travel the road not taken.

In my own case, I took advantage of a voluntary severance package offered by The Hamilton Spectator in 1996.

With nearly 17 years of service to my credit, the package was a sizeable sum that helped reduce some of the risk involved in establishing myself in the book writing and publishing field.

The buyout doubled my net worth and gave me some ready cash to live on while securing the financing for my last book, Success Stories, published in partnership with BRaSH Publishing.

After the book's release, I was ready for the next step. We dissolved the partnership; I founded Manor House Publishing. Enterprise 2000 was born.

Along the way, I also experienced working in the national media, first as an editor with the Globe & Mail, then with The Toronto Star where I continue to work as an editor/writer. During this time I've also worked as a contributing writer/editor to Marketing magazine and international periodicals.

Speaking from my own experience, even with all the risks involved, I still would have been far less happy if I had stayed at my old Spectator job.

It's a safe bet neither Success Stories nor Enterprise 2000 would have happened. And I would have been left forever wondering what it would be like to work in Toronto for two of the nation's biggest daily newspapers. I know I would never have left my somewhat comfortable rut without the buyout. Accepting it opened several doors of opportunity. Much higher-paying jobs, career advancement and personal satisfaction and achievement were all there for the taking. It's a move I'll never regret making.

But even if an employer offering little in the way of a financial cushion pushes you unwillingly out the door, you can still achieve success.

The odds are stacked heavily against you in such a scenario.

But the loss of employment is still accompanied by a newfound sense of freedom.Losing a job can sometimes be the best thing that could happen to you, unshackling you from a narrow way of thinking and opening up the possibility of success in another field.

Many young people entering the workforce will have to create their own jobs. They're being cast in the mold of the entrepreneur right from the start.

Obviously not everyone succeeds. But who can deny that amidst fear and uncertainty, the door to opportunity has been kicked wide open.

The situations I've just described fit a wide array of baby boomers who are being thrust willingly or unwillingly into the great wide open.

But for new generations of Canadians, the employment picture has been changed even more radically.

Many young people entering the workforce will have to create their own jobs. They're being cast in the mold of the entrepreneur right from the start.

Or, they may go to work for a company heavily involved in computers and the Internet, a firm likely run by a former classmate.

An example of such a start-up company is 701.com, an internet-based firm run by Greg Turkstra, son of well-known Hamilton lawyer Herman Turkstra. Although still very young, this company is creating a massive clientele of firms it provides with websites. The commercial possibilities seem endless and new opportunities are being created in this exciting new communications medium every day.

In fact, most of today's and tomorrow's graduates will work for companies that don't even exist today.

As many of these companies grow, new opportunities for advancement will follow. So will a wide variety of projects, plans and new ways of conducting business. The whole world is becoming steadily more interconnected and integrated.

Yes, while the future can indeed look frightening, you just have to get over the fear of the unknown to realize it can also be exhilarating, exciting, fascinating, filled with risk, adventure, surprises and opportunity.

In the New Age, computer literacy has become essential. Virtually all businesses depend on computers for at least part of their operation. Computers are essential, whether they're used to maintain customer and employee files, track shipments and inventories, perform accounting functions, do design work or dispense information.

Here again, the emphasis is on marketable skills. Access to jobs becomes greatly enhanced if you can operate computer programs with ease.

It's encouraging to realize that at Hillfield-Strathallan College, students are being taught to become computer literate at a young age and to be computer proficient by the time they leave the private high school.

At Appleby College, to further prepare students for the millennium, every classroom is wired for computers. All students are provided with IBM ThinkPad laptop computers.

And Junior Achievement provides many young people with invaluable business skills.

At the post-secondary level, matching education programs to job opportunities is the forte of Mohawk College of Applied Arts & Technology is emphasizing business ties and practical courses to forge success in an ever-changing work world.

Innovation is also part of the curriculum at Sheridan College.

Closing Notes: Limitless Horizons

Sheridan is the top pick for animation education in Canada, and one of the world's top three animation schools.

The Michael G. DeGroote School of Business at McMaster University is shaping new business leaders. It's living up to its motto: "Our graduates hit their career path running."

With their close ties to the business world, these various education institutions are well positioned to respond fast to marketplace changes.

And, of course, the BAC is playing an active part in "incubating" tomorrow's business leaders by cutting many of the costs that can cripple a start-up firm while providing a wealth of expert advice. The BAC's Entrepreneurial clients started up well over 600 businesses in mid 1990s, employing 860 people.

Throughout this book we've examined the role played by educational institutions, economic agencies and organizations and business leaders in shaping our economy, conquering change and paving the way for future generations.

We've also examined an economic region on the cusp of a new millennium. Together, Hamilton-Wentworth, Halton and Niagara comprise a vast economic zone encompassing more than 1 million people and a diversified economy.

Our regional economy will continue to diversify in the coming years, with high-technology companies playing a larger role as employers and net contributors to the area's wealth.

The nature of work will also continue to change through an accelerated evolution that will move even further away from the traditional employer concept to a model favouring contract agents, rather than employees, working from virtual or home-based offices rather office buildings.

Lee Kirkby, the former executive director of the Hamilton & District Chamber of Commerce, predicts a rise in the number of virtual corporations in which people offering various vital

Taking time to enjoy nature's splendour in Hamilton.

- Photo by Paul Sparrow

skills sets come together and function as a company to complete a given project. Once the project is completed, the "corporation" disbands.

"While the group is working together," Kirkby suggests, "they may appear to be much like any staff of people anywhere or they may be scattered all over the country, working out of their homes, linked together by computers and phone lines."

The Toronto Dominion Bank is predicting one million jobs will have been created during the three years leading up to the year 2000.

Despite uncertainties and an accelerated rate of change, the employment opportunities are vast.

Yet we can expect a continuation of two-income families as the norm, long work hours and further postponement of the promised Leisure Age.

It's important that we find the time to enjoy the fruits of our labour. As our young fisherman above shows, we live in a region of natural beauty.

Whatever we do in our quest to wrest success from the new economy, let's take some time to enjoy the old-fashioned splendour of Mother Nature.

- Michael B. Davie.

Index

Index

Enterprise 2000

Directory

Appleby College: (905) 845-4681

Beverly Tire
(905) 525-9240 or (888) 525-9240

Bick Financial Security:
(905) 648-9559

CKOC/K-Lite FM: (905) 574-1150

Columbia International College
(905) 572-7883

Country Chocolates: (519) 658-6268

M. G. DeGroote School of Business
(905) 525-9140 ext. 27634

Dining Lifestyles: (519) 473-8402

DOVE Marketing: (905) 529-3683

Eclipse Colour: (905) 634-1900

Edgewater Manor: (905) 643-9332

Dr. Roland Estrabillo: 387-2600

Garden Motorcar: (905) 523-5557

GT Associates: (905) 972-5772

Halton Business Development
(905) 825-6300

Hamilton Chamber of Commerce
(905) 522-1151

Hamilton Laser Eye Institute
(888) 636-4733 or (905) 388-9505

Hamilton Economic Development
(905) 546-4447

Heddle Marine: (905) 528-2635

Hillfield-Strathallan: (905) 389-1367

IRD1: (905) 646-8855

Jerry Santucci, Berkshire Group
(905) 319-9000

Junior Achievement: (905) 528-5252

Leppert Business Systems
(905) 522-9029

Dr. Tony Mancuso: (905) 734-9901

Market Matters: (905) 561-2560

McKeil Marine: (905) 528-4780

Mohawk College: (905) 575-2131

Micro-Aide: (905) 574-1995

Mr. Mugs Coffee: (519) 752-9890

Niagara Economic/Tourism Corp.
(905) 685-1308

Niagara Land Co./Vineland Estates
(905) 562-7088

ONtv: (905) 645-2071

Paul Sparrow, Photographer
(905) 523-5665

Reimer Construction
(905) 336-8775

Royal Connaught: (905) 546-8111

Sheraton Hamilton: (905) 529-5515

Sheridan College: (905) 845-9430

E.D. Smith & Sons: (905) 643-1211

Stirling Print-All: (905) 525-5467

Tim Donut Limited: (905) 845-6511

A.D. Vacca & Associates
(905) 549-7526

Westbury International
(905) 335-8533

Patrons

A Happy Day Limousine Service

B. Jonathan Banfield
Painting & Decorating

Ron and June Cleave

Paul and Linda Cleave

Country Chocolates, Cambridge

Cameron and Michele Fraser Davie

Randy and Gay Davie

Kirby and Roxanne Davie

Pearl and Robert Davie

De Feo's Auto Service Limited

Wanda Dzierzbicki

Eclipse Colour

The Effort Trust Company

Randy and Elizabeth Guitard

Joynt Ventures

Richard and Eleanor Kosydar

Dr. Sean P. McDonough, Dentist

Micro Aide Computer Services

Mohawk College
of Applied Arts & Technology

Rai Puder

Royal Connaught
Howard Johnson Plaza Hotel

Toronto Dominion Bank, Hamilton
James & Robinson Branch

WMD Consultants

Laura and Frank Wysocki